More Than
Meets the Eye

More Than Meets the Eye

The Story of a Remarkable Life and a Transcending Love

Joan Brock and Derek L. Gill

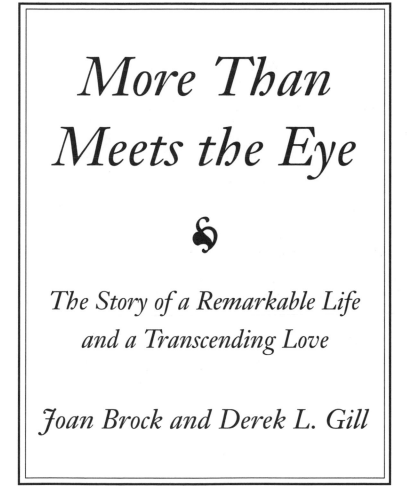

HarperCollins*Publishers*

HarperCollins books may be purchased for educational, business, or sales promotional use. For information, please write: Special Markets Department, HarperCollins Publishers, Inc., 10 East 53rd Street, New York, NY 10022.

FIRST EDITION

Designed by George J. McKeon

LIBRARY OF CONGRESS CATALOGING-IN-PUBLICATION DATA

Brock, Joan, 1952–
   More Than Meets the Eye/by Joan Brock and Derek L. Gill—1st ed.
   p. cm.
   ISBN 0-06-017609-1
   1. Brock, Joan, 1952–. 2. Blind—United States—Biography.
 I. Gill, Derek L. T. II. Title.
 HV1792.B83A3 1994
362.4'1'092—dc20   94-4863
[B]

94 95 96 97 98 ❖/RRD 10 9 8 7 6 5 4 3 2 1

To Joy and Jay

In memoriam to Joe and my father

Contents

❧

Acknowledgments

§

In loving gratitude to Jim and my mother; also Bob, Jon, my extended family, and Joe's extended family. Thanks especially to Derek Gill, Tom Sullivan, Elspeth Nickerson, Bruce Gallaudet, Brenda Peterson, and editor Buz Wyeth; the staff and students of the Iowa Braille and Sight Saving School; the physicians and other members of the healing arts for their skill and care. How grateful I am, too, for the love, laughter, shared tears, and prayers of those special friends—they know who they are—who have touched my life over both the darker and the sun-filled times. Special thanks, too, to Mr. and Mrs. Leonard Van Doorn and Mr. and Mrs. Ron Lehr, whose generosity helped me to write this book.

Above all, thanks to God for his "Amazing Grace."

Introducing Joan

§

That I played a role in creating this book gives me both extraordinary pleasure and pride. For not only is it a story of compelling drama—indeed many readers will ignore the clock until they've traveled from cover to cover—but for me (and here I speak as a musician) it is as haunting as a love song.

Within one of the chapters Joan Brock speaks of the time when I first encountered her. Very obviously, as will be understood, we had, importantly, something in common. However, I became aware immediately that this lovely woman (and we'll speak of her beauty momentarily) had a unique and enthralling story to tell.

How many songs have died because the lyrics have not melded with the music, and how many good tales have been lost in the telling? After Joan had spoken to me about the incredible experiences of her still young life, I saw that her need was to find a professional who could help her write from the heart as well as from the head. Fortuitously, a best-selling author is among the closest of my friends. Derek Gill worked with me in telling the story of my boyhood and early adult years.

As those old-time professional matchmakers gained personal gratification from arranging an ideal mating, so I now have my reward from being instrumental in the prospering of this literary partnership.

Thus Joan, with her wonderful personal story, and Derek with his experienced pen, have created a book which will, I believe, inspire many to dare distant horizons which they might have thought to be beyond their attainment, beyond their courage and faith. And what challenging and exhilarating voyaging!

I have not seen Joan. Indeed, I've not seen anyone or anything. My wife, Patty, and others have told me that she is strikingly beautiful. But I do know of her radiance which illuminates the hearts of all who meet her.

The reader of *More Than Meets the Eye* will also glow from Joan's inner radiance, and will be reminded that in her own words, "not only darkness but dawn" is also heralded by twilight.

Tom Sullivan

1

Winter's Twilight

§

E ven had it not been the day before my thirty-second birthday, I could never forget the date. On awakening that morning I was quite unaware that the compass of my life had begun to
swing radically.

I had a smidgen of concern about a slight headache and a
mild sense of lassitude. Oh gosh! I thought, hope I'm not in for a
cold—oh, please, not in this weather.

After showering, I used the sleeve of my gown to wipe steam
from the bathroom window. This enabled me to read the outside
thermometer. It showed twenty degrees below zero. I shivered
and indulged in covetous thoughts about California, where I had
grown up. I enjoyed recollected images of palm trees and golden
beaches. My husband, Joe, was already downstairs and doubtless
hungry for breakfast.

I peeked through the door of Joy's room. Our three-year-old was still asleep, her golden hair spread across the pillow and her eyeless teddy bear limply clasped above the covers.

Once I had gotten Joe out of the house there would be time enough to stir and dress our daughter.

Life for Joe and me was more than satisfying. It was rewarding at the deepest level because both of us really loved our professional work at the Iowa Braille and Sight Saving School. Joe was the director of leisure and recreational training and I was responsible for liaison between dorm parents and classroom teachers. I was also involved with the school's public relations. Even when our schedules overlapped, Joy was always close at hand because her preschool classroom was on the Braille School's campus. I cannot recall contemplating the smallest shadow of worry about the future.

The reason for Joe's early departure from home that morning was that he went to a basketball game with his friends before work. He would be back to pick up Joy and me shortly after nine o'clock. Joy and I had an unhurried pancake breakfast and then it was time to get her dressed.

Our daughter was showing early sign of independence. She bounced around her bedroom, gathering a blouse here, pants there, underwear from under her Cabbage Patch dolls (what on earth were they doing there?), a padded snowsuit, a thick scarf from behind the door. As usual, the business of getting all these garments on her in the right order was all squirms and squeaks. The task completed, she looked like a brown-eyed stuffed doll who could still move, but only barely. All she needed to cope with the outside temperature was a cap with earflaps and boots, both down in the hall, and socks—ah, yes, socks!

I pulled out the second dresser drawer and pursed my lips.

"Pumpkin, what's happened to your pink socks?" I asked.

Joy waddled across to the dresser where she stood on her toes. This allowed her to tip her nose over the top of the opened drawer. Then she pointed.

"There they are, Mommy—there in the corner. Lots of them."

I followed the direction of her finger. "But those are white," I said.

An impatient sigh from Joy. "Oh, Mommy, they're pink, pink, pink, like my pants."

She could not quite reach the pair she was indicating so I pulled them out myself. I studied them closely. They were white. Joy went back to the bed, her feet in the air waiting for me to put on the selected socks. I went to the Winnie-the-Pooh lamp and very slowly turned the socks over in my hand. There was no trace of color at all.

"What are you waiting for?" squeaked the stuffed doll from the bed.

"I—er—are you sure these are pink?"

Another deep sigh from Joy. "Oh, Mommy, don't be silly. You're going to make me late for school."

I closed my eyes and rubbed them, then looked again. The color hadn't changed. I swallowed. Gnats of worry buzzed across my mind. This was absurd. Maybe the incipient cold or my sinuses are playing tricks on me, I thought. Anyway, I heard the car in the driveway so there was no time to argue further. By the time I had Joy fully dressed, Joe was stomping the snow off his boots at the kitchen door.

Joy leaped into his arms and in moments we were on our way to the campus. Joe was aglow from his exercise and murmured something about having dropped nearly ten pounds in the past three weeks. Joe was built like a refrigerator and was in a permanent state of war with the bathroom scales.

"Didn't you hear me?" he asked. "Nearly ten pounds!"

"Great," I responded without adequate enthusiasm.

The brilliance of the snow dazzled my eyes.

"Something on your mind?" asked Joe.

The car was slowing for a stop sign. "Yes," I said. "What color are Joy's socks?"

"For Pete's sake!" he exclaimed. "I thought that at least you'd clogged the kitchen sink again."

The car had stopped. "I'm serious," I said. "Just check the color, please."

He glanced at me, his brow furrowed. Then he swiveled around and asked Joy, in the backseat, to lift her pants cuffs. Before replying, he moved the car across the intersection.

Then, with mock gravity, he said: "The news this morning is that the President is expected to make an important new statement about the Panama Canal. There was an airplane hijacking in Greece. Another blizzard is sweeping down from Canada." A pause. "And our daughter is wearing a pair of pink socks." He guffawed.

I didn't even smile as I felt another small stab of concern.

The journey through the little town of Vinton was a short one. The current joke was that the birth of triplets to the Mifflin family had pushed the population up over the five thousand mark. Boastfully, it was the county seat and, at Christmastime, folks drove in from places a hundred miles away to see the tree-lined streets and red-bricked public buildings sparkling with lights. It was a community full of friends, I mean that one was on first-name terms with the mailman and the grocery clerks. Many folks didn't even bother to lock their doors at night, and the cops were more likely to wave admonishing fingers than give tickets when they caught you driving ten miles over the speed limit. If you were down with the flu, neighbors dropped in with an apple strudel and grandmother's herbal potion. It was a community where church pews were filled on Sunday and where people gave generously of their time and treasure to worthwhile causes. Vinton was just the right place for a school for blind kids.

On my schedule for that day was an afternoon talk to a women's association. I hoped to recruit volunteers to help kids with one-on-one assistance. I relished talking about "my kids" and their special needs.

Joe, the powerfully built man at my side whose secret ambition was to be a shooting guard in the National Basketball Association, was adored by the sightless children.

He stopped the car near Joy's preschool. He leaned over and gave each of us a peck. "Well, here we are, lover girl," he said to Joy, and to me he said, "Good luck with your presentation."

Joy and I gripped gloved hands to walk across the street. A wintry sun was shining directly at us and the snow was so bright that I made my eyes into slits. Joy was prattling on about her friend, Susie, when I suddenly lurched forward. I had tripped over a curbside mound of snow.

"Oh, Mommy!" exclaimed Joy in alarm. "Didn't you see it?"

"No, I guess I didn't," I said breathlessly.

But a moment later I stumbled again.

I looked back. With the sunlight now behind me I could clearly see why I had tripped because the mounds of snow threw shadows onto the road. Yet the moment I turned to move toward the sunlight the landscape flattened out. It was quite puzzling—but no more than that.

Before Joy and I parted at the preschool door she more than

compensated for my clumsiness and concern. She looked up at me and said solemnly, "Mommy, you look so pretty today." I gave her a hug.

When I reached my own office, Joy's heartwarming valediction was one reason I bypassed my desk and made straight for the rest room.

Looking back at me from the mirror was certainly a face I recognized, except that I looked so pale. Figuring that a little more blush would correct the problem I pulled out my compact. My hand froze between compact and cheek. The blush looked like talcum powder.

I took the compact to the window, but the natural light did not change the white color to a roseate hue. I took several deep breaths. There had to be an explanation. It was eerie. Was it, I pondered, a sort of snow blindness—just a temporary thing that inconvenienced the guys who skied without darkened goggles? Wasn't the treatment just a few hours in a dark room and lots of orange juice? Something like that.

In heading for my office I passed the staff secretary, Ione, at her desk. She gave me her usual greeting, "Hi, Joan, how are you today?"

I stopped and turned to her. "Well, truthfully, not so hot," I said. "Think I'm getting a cold. Do I look okay to you?"

Ione gave me a second glance. "Fine," she said, "except—well . . . "

"Well, what?" I asked sharply.

She laughed with embarrassment. "You're wearing enough makeup to play the clown at a children's party." She whipped a tissue from her purse and stood up. "May I try to improve things?"

I forced a smile. "Please go ahead. I was in a hurry this morning."

She tossed away the stained Kleenex. "There," she said, smiling, "now you look like the refined and lovely young woman that you are. The ladies you'll be speaking to this afternoon will be properly impressed." She turned back to her desk. "You're one of the lucky ones who doesn't really need much makeup."

Her easy laugh eased my tension. From the day I joined the school's staff, Ione had been one of those naturally supportive people whose friendship I much valued. While I was working on my lecture notes she came to my office and noticed me rubbing my eyes. She suggested that if I really had a bug I should go home. She offered to get a message to Joe and to pick up Joy from the preschool. I declined these suggestions and told her I'd be fine, yet I couldn't stop thinking about Joy's socks.

The rest of my day went well. I took a couple of classes with the kids (to whom it mattered not whether I looked like a ghost or a clown), attended an administrative meeting in the late afternoon, and met with the ladies of the church group, who gave me a warm welcome. I managed to sign up another half dozen volunteers.

By the time I collected Joy, the wintry sun was setting. In the fading light my eyesight improved. I could definitely mark the undulations in the snow. On the way home I stopped in at a pharmacy, intending only to buy over-the-counter medication for my cold. I did purchase some recommended capsules, but on the way to the exit I noticed a rack of sunglasses. I tried on a pair. Everything looked much clearer. I bought the glasses too.

Joe was amused by the glasses, flashed a big grin, and asked if I had any Hollywood pretensions. "Don't those female film stars wear sunglasses even in bed?" he joked.

"How would you know?" I parried. Joe's grin widened. Then I tried to explain that the dark glasses helped a lot. But by this time I'd understandably lost his attention because there was a sports program on the TV.

The next day all the trillion cold bugs made a full-scale attack. I felt awful. My head throbbed like an African drum. I phoned the Braille School to tell them I wouldn't be in, and why. I was actually talking to Brenda Armstrong, another colleague and close friend. When I had outlined my symptoms and related how pink socks looked white, Brenda immediately advised me to see my doctor.

"Oh, it's not that bad," I protested.

Brenda said, "Perhaps not, but I don't like what you're telling me. Get to a doctor now—as soon as possible, like today, if you can."

The urgency in Brenda's voice got to me. She had joined the Braille School staff at the same time I had. She was a professional authority on educating people with low or no vision. I asked myself if she knew something about my visual aberration that I didn't.

"Okay," I told Brenda, trying to keep my voice casual, "I'll try to get an appointment today."

"Good girl. And by the way," she added, "isn't it your birthday?"

"That's the problem," I sniffed. "We've got Joe's brother and his wife coming. They're taking us out to dinner."

"Congratulations," she said, "but keep your priorities in order."

In fact, the doctor's appointments' ledger was already overloaded, or so his assistant told me. However, she could squeeze me in early the following morning.

That evening, when we went out to Vinton's plushest steak house with Joe's kinfolk, I assuredly wasn't an Emily Post. But I got through the evening and also half a box of tissues. Birthday kisses were sensibly postponed.

The following morning I was Dr. Tony Anthony's first patient. He greeted me warmly because not only was he the official physician for the Braille School, he was also a good friend.

His first question was why on earth I was wearing dark glasses on a January morning. I explained how the glasses helped me to see a whole lot better outside in the snow-blanketed community, and how they also helped me under the bright lights of his office. Then I laughingly told him the story of Joy's socks.

He reached out and removed my glasses. "Okay, Joan," he demanded, "what color is this room?"

I squinted at the walls. "Pretty close to being the same color as the ceiling," I said guardedly.

"Which is?"

"White, of course."

"Not quite," said the doctor.

I looked at the walls again. "Well," I conceded, "I suppose they could be a little off-white. Out west they might call it adobe white."

Dr. Anthony chewed his lip.

I asked, "They're not by any chance . . . "

"Yes they are." He grunted. "The decorator's choice, not mine, I assure you. But they are very patently a deep shade of pink."

I was aware of a missed heartbeat. The doctor rose from his desk and went to the door. Over his shoulder he told me that he would be sending in his assistant to make routine tests, including a check on eye pressure.

He must have observed my look of concern. He came back, patted both shoulders and said, "We're going to find out what the trouble is. It may well be sinusitis. There's a lot around at this time of year." His hands slipped up to my neck. "Glands swollen," he added.

Routine checks by the assistant took quite a long time. My ears and throat were examined, my blood pressure taken, my eyes numbed by drops of anesthetic for the eye pressure test. I was recalling how the kids in my classes at school regularly took similar tests. I'd often accompanied them, held their hands, comforted them. And now it was me in the chair! I needed someone to hold my hand.

As I sat alone waiting for the return of Tony Anthony, the mild anxieties of the past forty-eight hours began to coalesce into a clot of fear.

But no, I told myself, there can't possibly be anything seriously wrong. I had twenty-twenty vision. I didn't need glasses for the phone directory, and when migrating geese flew over Vinton I was the first to spot them. Except for this darned cold I felt pretty good. Anyway, no one's eyesight deteriorated overnight—not insofar as I knew—unless there'd been an explosion or something. There was that one kid at the school, poor little Harry, who'd lost his sight fairly rapidly. But that was after a car accident, or was it a fireworks accident—something like that.

But no matter how hard I tried to soar on thermals of optimism, the fears began to spiral into panic. I did have one fail-safe answer to panic.

I prayed (in a whisper, as I recall), "Dear Lord, you know what's wrong—if there's anything wrong—but please take away my fear."

Almost instantly, my hunched shoulders dropped and my fisted fingers uncurled. Truly, the sudden, scary squall within my mind quietened. A moment later the door opened, and in came Dr. Anthony and his assistant.

He said breezily, "Joan, the eye pressure checks out just fine, but this visual loss of color is—er—confusing. So I want you to see an ophthalmologist."

"But isn't my cold causing the problem?" I suggested.

"May well be," he replied. "But—well—it could be more serious."

"Serious! But you said my eyes were okay."

"No, I didn't say that. I said the pressure was within the norms."

"But wouldn't a couple of days in bed, and—"

Dr. Anthony cut in. "I've already been on the phone. You've got an appointment to see a good man in Waterloo this very afternoon."

Ten minutes later I was back home. Joe and Joy were dressed for the winter's blast and ready to take off for the preschool and his office.

"Heck, you were a long time," said Joe. "Was the waiting room that full?"

Joy asked, "Mommy, did they give you a shot?"

I gave her a smile. "No shot, but I'm afraid we're going to have to reorganize the day. I've got to be in Waterloo by two o'clock. I've got to see an eye doctor."

"Whoopee! No school!" exclaimed Joy.

Joe gave me a keen look. Crisply, he said, "I'll phone the office."

While we were driving, Joy asked me to read to her. Because my eyes were watery I suggested we recite nursery rhymes. We singsonged "Jack and Jill went up the hill," and "Little Jack Horner sat in a corner." Her favorite was "The Snowflake Song." Together, and for the umpteenth time, we sang "The Snowflake Song":

For goodness, goodness sakes,
Just look at all those snowflakes!
Ping, pong, pung!
I'll catch some on my tongue.

Like the petals of a rose
They're landing on my nose.
Pung, pong, ping!
Snow makes me want to sing!

Snow's coming down in whirls,
Flakes landing on my curls!
Ping, pung, pong!
This is my snowflake song!

It was a timely verse, because the blizzard that had been forecast kept the windshield wipers working at the maximum pace. After the second encore Joe joined in. For the next few miles, "The Snowflake Song" and our laughter helped me to forget completely the need for the journey.

In now recalling that drive down the white-ribboned road between Vinton and Waterloo I can recreate the scenes with quite extraordinary vividness. I see the whirling of snowflakes. I hear the squeaking of windshield wipers working overtime to give some vision through the blizzard. My nostrils even pick up the pungent smell of damp woolen scarves and mittens. I hear again our chorus of laughter as though, long years ago, I had made a high-fidelity recording of it.

I know now, of course, why the picture is so clear, why the kaleidoscope of sounds and scents and touch are so deeply grooved upon my mind. What I did not comprehend at the time was that soon, so very soon, the harmony of all my senses would not experience the like again.

2

"That's My Wife!"

The Waterloo ophthalmologist dilated my eyes and spent a long time peering through a sophisticated apparatus. Joe and Joy remained in the waiting room.

Eventually the doctor swiveled his chair around to a wall desk. His pen scratched on a notepad. My patience had rarely been more hard-tested. My mind was screaming *Tell me I'm going to be okay! Tell me something!*

The scratching of the pen ceased. The doctor stood up. Disappointingly he said, "Let's go to my office."

Once again I find myself recalling small and irrelevant details of this the first of many expert examinations of my eyes. I remember the exceptionally deep pile of the office carpet, the backs of what seemed to be silver photograph frames on the desk. I can see again what appeared to be an India-ink etching or sketch of a seascape on the wall above the doctor's head. It may have been a colorful painting. Somewhere behind me a clock faintly ticked away the seconds.

Through misting eyes, I could make out that the doctor was turning pages of a large, presumably medical volume. I kneaded the smooth armrests of the chair.

"Tick-tock" went the clock as seconds mounted into one minute, two minutes. I felt I knew what it was like to be in the dock of a courtroom when the jury had just returned with a verdict.

"Guilty or innocent?" I heard myself asking.

I could make out the doctor lifting his face from the volume and removing his spectacles.

"What was that?" he asked.

My voice again—like a mendicant pleading for alms. "Please, doctor, give me something. Give me the verdict."

The heavy volume was closed with the sound of a wet towel being dropped on a bathroom floor, a sort of plop. His answer was about as anticlimactic as it could be. "I don't know," he said.

"You don't know?" I exclaimed. "But there must be something, there must . . . "

"Yes, Mrs. Beringer, there is obviously something. But without more tests, for which I don't have the facilities, I cannot tell you what the problem is."

Then he gave me a short lecture on what he described as "the astonishing miracle" of eyesight. He spoke as if he were talking to a child. He told me that the retina of each eye holds 107 million cells. Of these, 7 million are cones, each electrically charged to send off messages to the brain the moment a few photons of light strike them. The cones provide color awareness. They provide the ability to distinguish a thousand shades of color.

"The cones are the cells which, when healthy, should have told you that your daughter's socks were pink, not white." He chuckled over my recalling that story for him.

I helped him along. I was now anxious to rejoin Joe and Joy. I interjected, "And the rods distinguish between black and white."

"Quite right," he said enthusiastically, as if he were a teacher congratulating a bright student. "I was forgetting that you work with blind children. Guess you've studied these things. Yes, the rods pick out shades of gray. They allow you to see, for instance, shapes on a moonlit night."

Through the door and somewhere down the passage I could hear Joy's laughter. I figured that she had to have found something funny in a comic book. The doctor continued his mini-lecture, but now he upgraded my intelligence and threw in a few polysyllabic words.

"As I was saying, Mrs. Beringer, there's obviously some neurological interference to your visual capacity—markedly, to the reception of the cones. Frankly, I do not know why, so I am referring you to an appropriate specialist at the University of Iowa Hospital. As a matter of fact, he's a friend, so I'm sure they'll give you an early appointment and find the answers."

"And the cure?" I asked.

He stood up, came around the desk, and patted my arm. "Why not?" he said. "Diagnostically they're making big strides. Find the cause, then find the cure. That's what we physicians are trained for."

On my returning to the waiting room I felt sure Joe could tell from my expression that I was not yet ready to celebrate anything.

It was, in fact, two weeks before I could get an appointment at the University of Iowa Hospital. When I awakened each morning I hoped that my eyes would be better, but each day my vision was worse. I tried to convince myself that I could function adequately. I had been driving Joy the two and a half blocks to her preschool. The windshield became more and more fogged up. I vainly tried to clean the glass.

One morning, bitter as it was, I opened the window and stuck out my head, hoping that I'd be able to see better. The fog was still there. I drove over a deep gutter, causing the car to rock wildly and bump hard. Joy cried out in alarm. I acknowledged that I was endangering my daughter and others on the road. I somehow managed to deliver Joy to the preschool; then I deserted the car and stumbled through the snow to Joe's office.

To Joe I blurted out, "I cannot drive again. I could have killed Joy this morning or maybe run down another child. I must not drive anymore. I'm so sorry, Joe. Forgive me."

He was gentle with me. "There is nothing to forgive," he told me. "They'll find the problem. They'll find the answer." He said this with real and comforting conviction.

Colleagues at the school were no less sympathetic, no less helpful. My supervisor, Dan Wirth, who was director of student/home services, gave me a magnifying device, in size and shape like a golf ball, but flattened at the top and bottom. When placed on a page, he told me, it would magnify letters fivefold.

One late afternoon after I'd been working, I took the device to the deserted school library, a handsome building that housed many Braille books, technical books, and shelves of large-print books for the partially blind. The sun was setting and the light in the empty library was low—a light that now best suited me.

I took one of the large-print books to a corner desk, then placed the magnifying glass to a page randomly selected. I couldn't make out a single letter, let alone a word. I turned the glass golf ball the other way round and tried again. All that was visible were faint blobs.

A brutal truth hit me with crushing impact. My central vision was all but gone. Many of the partially blind children could see better than I could now see.

"Oh God! Oh God!" I cried the words aloud in the silent library. Tears welled up and fell upon the hand that held the golf ball magnifying glass.

The almost eerie quiet was broken by the sound of approaching footsteps. A stairwell door was opened with a rattle of keys. A janitor was making his rounds. The library door was swung open but the janitor did not see me at the corner desk. His footsteps faded into silence. Now another fearful truth: my ears were becoming as important to me as my eyes. As twilight moved to darkness, I remained at the desk too numbed to move until I remembered that Joe was to meet me in the entrance lobby downstairs. My limbs jerked into action, for were Joe to see no lights from the library windows he would assume I'd made my own way home.

When we met in the lobby I collapsed into Joe's arms. His rebuke stopped my slide into hysteria.

"Snap out of it, Joan," he told me. "You've got to shape up and start to take a positive attitude. Isn't that what we teach them in this place?"

I sobbed, "But I couldn't read a single word." I held the glass golf ball out to him. "It didn't work. Just blurs. Nothing."

He put an arm around my shoulders. "People don't go blind—not just like that. It doesn't happen that way, and you know it."

That's right, I told myself. It doesn't happen like that. I couldn't think of one child who had come into my care who had

had a medical history comparable to what seemed to be happening to me.

As we walked from the library to the car, I repeated Joe's words aloud. "You're right," I said, "it doesn't happen like that. It doesn't! It doesn't!"

What was curious and initially encouraging, too, was that I still had some peripheral vision. In brilliant light I was almost totally blind, but when the light was low I could, if I turned my head, make out objects, albeit colorless, and movement. There were moments, too, again when the light was dim or when I was wearing dark glasses (which I now did most of the time), when I rediscovered a tiny window of central vision.

So I was not without hope when Joe and I set out for my first appointment at the University of Iowa Hospital in Iowa City. It is one of the biggest teaching hospitals in America and it was only an hour's drive from Vinton.

The hospital's ophthalmology department was familiar to me, for I'd often taken Braille School children there. I knew that I'd be going to an institution that had not only the latest diagnostic equipment, but several specialists with national and even international reputations. I was consoled by knowing that in seeking the cause and cure of my problem the best medical help was virtually on my doorstep.

I was hardly less fortunate in being on the staff of Vinton's Braille and Sight Saving School, where many of my co-workers were highly trained and long experienced in helping the blind and partially sighted cope with their totally dark or shadowed worlds.

As we turned onto the highway for Iowa City, I mentioned these advantages to Joe. I said laughingly, "If there's one place I'd choose to be blind it's right here!"

I was shaken by his almost savage response. He thumped the

steering wheel with his fist and said, "For Pete's sake, Joan, it's not funny. Anyway, you're not going blind, damn it! You can't!"

In the ensuing silence I began to comprehend what a load I had placed upon my husband. I felt sure he had already pictured himself with a blind wife and, because he was a perfectionist, the picture would be grim, perhaps intolerable. As a gesture of reassurance, I wanted to reach out and touch his arm, but feelings of guilt and resentment held me back.

The tension became an almost physical barrier and, as I was soon to discover, silence and isolation can so readily provide an atmosphere for negative thinking.

As we drove to Iowa City I found myself reflecting upon the irony of my situation. Here I was, a professional, a mother and a wife who, just a few weeks earlier, had been contented enough with her life. Each day I had been giving my physical, mental, and spiritual energy to helping children scramble and claw their way up from their own dark pits into a world of sighted people. I had had the privilege of assisting children in their journey from helplessness to achievement, from self-defeat to self-confidence. I had had a real and rewarding part in helping young people move with a sense of promise into an illuminated environment.

But was I myself now going the other way? Was I slithering into dark valleys, tumbling, and out of control of my own destiny . . . ?

It was a horrible thought, but a worse one followed. Shamefully there flashed through my mind the possibility that some blindness could be contagious or infectious. Had I, in hugging one of my blind children—and, God knows, no one is in more need of hugging—picked up some bug that was causing my loss of sight? I killed this completely irrational thought immediately, for I knew that were I to pursue it, the only end result would be bitterness.

As Joe turned the car into the parking lot of the huge hospital I resolved that were I ever again to blame anyone else for what was happening to me I would crush the notion at once.

When Joe opened the car door for me I must have been smiling, for he apologized for what he called "my loss of perspective." "Okay, Joan, let's get to these guys who are going to fix you up." A grim laugh, then, "Yeah, if they don't fix you up good they're going to have to answer to me!"

I now understood what really troubled Joe. This man at my shoulder who gave every outward impression that he was afraid of nothing or anyone was now, in fact, fearful. He was afraid for me, afraid for Joy, and, I was sure, afraid for himself.

In facing up to his own fears he had convinced himself that I was going to get well. What right had I to question this conviction?

Our reception was hardly red-carpet. We were merely one couple in a myriad of people—grandparents hobbling, babies crying, a family within earshot obviously grieving. My guess was that the young woman at the reception desk to which we were directed had either just had a fight with her boyfriend or was suffering from PMS. She was coldly brusque as she tapped into her computer the usual questions and answers. I could almost see Joe's greenest gall rising when she demanded evidence of health insurance before she would type in my name.

Then we had to find our way to the ophthalmology department which, I could recall, was about a mile distant, or so it seemed. As we dodged between other patients, gurneys, visitors, and unidentifiable others, Joe grumbled that the hospital should have installed a Disneyland-like monorail.

At last we reached the appropriate waiting room. My fuzzy vision indicated that at least three dozen people had arrived there ahead of us. Then the waiting—and the waiting and the waiting.

These times of waiting were to be among the worst for me, perhaps the worst for many patients entering a hospital, each confused, each wondering what had gone wrong with their bodies; many hurting, many scared.

It was nearly two hours after my scheduled appointment when my name was called. Joe was not with me at this moment. He had left the room to find a water fountain. I stood up and, for better vision, glanced sideways, fuzzily, to see what appeared to be an immensely tall man beckoning me. I followed his white coat until we reached another room where other white-coated individuals were grouped together.

I was taken to a chair that could have been a prop for a *Star Wars* movie—or could have been cannibalized from furniture in a hair-dressing salon or a dentist's office. There seemed to be a Viking-like helmet above my head. If I had not been anxious about Joe I would have been tempted to call out, "Beam me up, Scotty!"

Then I was aware that Joe had arrived. One of the white coats (female) asked if he was lost; what he was doing in this area?

"That's my wife," said Joe, "and I'm staying with her." He spoke with the authority of a Marine colonel. I could see him move to an empty seat. I gave him a grateful smile.

The very tall doctor squatted on a stool beside me. He said so wearily that I guessed I was probably his tenth patient since his working day had begun, "Now, Mrs. Beringer, will you please read the third line down on the chart on the wall in front of you."

"What chart?" I asked. My question created a sudden silence. Although I couldn't be sure, I felt that every white coat in the room was staring at me.

3

The White Coats

§

On that first visit to the University of Iowa Hospital, between fifteen and twenty physicians and medical students took turns studying my eyes. It was awful. The white coats, as I collectively called them, seemed to regard me with very special interest. What not only irritated me, and offended Joe greatly, was that they often talked about my case as if I wasn't within earshot. To me, most of the exchanges were medical gobbledygook, but I translated enough to comprehend that what they were seeing through their ophthalmoscopes was most unusual.

Whenever I asked questions I was patronized. "We'll let you know in good time," said one white coat. "We're still working on it," said another. "Just be patient, Mrs. Beringer," said a third.

The name of one doctor kept cropping up, and it was spoken with reverence. Dr. James Corbett was the chief of neuro-ophthalmology. I was given to understand that all the reports on my eye examinations were being referred to him. The order came through from Dr. Corbett that I was to have an immediate CAT scan.

Joe could see how exhausted I was from three hours of examinations, and I feared he might blow his top when told about the CAT scan, which, we understood, would take about one hour.

It was not until very late in the afternoon and after the scan that I first met Dr. Corbett. Joe was at my side when we were taken to his office.

"So this is the famous Joan Beringer," he said as he shook my hand.

"Famous!" I responded with surprise. "Oh, no, not me. You must be thinking of another patient."

Dr. Corbett chuckled, and several white coats who were standing nearby chuckled along with him. "Young lady," he said, "you've been keeping much of my staff busy today and you're a real puzzlement."

One of the white coats interjected, "Indeed, we're all very intrigued. Not come across anything quite like it. We're like astronomers picking up strange signals and we're going to train our most powerful—er—telescopes on the—er—object."

I could sense that Joe was beginning to seethe again. The astronomy metaphor had, unwittingly, not been well chosen. Joe had protested several times in the course of this long day that I was being treated like an object. I nudged his arm and hoped he would pick up the signal to bite his tongue.

"Ah, but we haven't given you the good news, Mrs. Beringer," said Dr. Corbett.

Good news! A surge of relief began to sweep over me.

From Joe's next remark it was obvious that he, too, now felt that the worst was over and that my loss of sight was temporary. I was aware of his chest expanding with a huge intake of breath. He blew out most of the air with a long, drawn-out "Pheeew" and then said, "Well, thank heavens for that! Can we go home now?"

"Afraid you've misunderstood me," said Dr. Corbett quickly. "I was speaking about the CAT scan. The images show no signs of a brain tumor."

My mind was now reeling. Tumor! I'd never given any thought to my having a brain tumor. No one had even whispered that that was what they'd been looking for when they'd given me a CAT scan.

Joe snorted. "So that's what you call good news, doctor!"

Dr. Corbett responded coolly. "It is good news. There seemed to be indications—the speed of the onset of the loss of vision, for instance—which suggested possibilities of a tumor. Yes, we're much relieved, Mr. Beringer, but we want to continue with other tests at once. Your wife's to be admitted to the hospital immediately."

My knees felt rubbery. I leaned heavily on Joe's arm. "Oh no," I said weakly. "I can't possibly. We have a small daughter at home. We've got to—"

Dr. Corbett cut in. He said quietly, "I think you don't understand how concerned we are and how determined we are to find the cause of the problem. I've already given instructions for your next major test—a spinal tap at eight tomorrow morning."

Protectively, perhaps, Joe moved half a pace in front of me. With that ring to his voice that could bring a sassy student to heel he said, "Five minutes from now my wife and I are going to be on our way to our home in Vinton. She's had one heck of a day here, and she's going to have a restful night in her bed—in our bed. If you insist, I'll get here by seven o'clock tomorrow morning."

A pause, then, "Fair enough," said Dr. Corbett. I felt sure I heard a collective sigh from the other white coats. Clearly no one ever questioned the orders of Dr. Corbett—no one except Joe. I was proud of him.

My husband was already leading me away when, over a shoulder, I asked the doctor, "Do I need to bring anything with me—a toothbrush, whatever?"

A laugh from everyone. Dr. Corbett said, "A toothbrush, certainly, and enough toothpaste to last you at least two weeks."

"Two weeks!" I exclaimed. "I'm not feeling sick or anything."

Dr. Corbett put his hand on my shoulder. He said, "May I call you Joan? We're going to be seeing a lot of each other. Yes, I'm afraid at least two weeks. We're planning a lot of tests."

When we reached home, one of my first duties was to call our folks. I had previously told them in rather vague terms that I was having trouble with my eyes, but now it was time to speak of the gravity of my condition.

Mom and Dad lived in Wisconsin where Dad had his present ministry. Dad was a pastor of the Reformed Church in the United States. Joe's parents, Ken and JoAnne, lived in South Dakota. Both couples were about six driving hours away. To all four of them we gave just the basic facts. Dad and Joe's parents insisted on being with us as soon as possible. They would be on the road before dawn. Joe's folks would take over when needed.

Joy was excited by the prospect of seeing her grandparents, but was confused by my inability to read to her.

Joy was not yet four, and I felt, as did Joe, that it was not the right moment to explain my vision loss. As I tucked her into bed, I told her simply that I would not be at home for a while because I had to go to the hospital. I assured her that she could come and see me. It would be the first time in her life that we would be parted for more than a few hours.

Joy mulled over this information for a few moments. I was wrong in anticipating protests and tears, and delighted when she asked, "Can we ask God to help you, Mommy?"

Joy's prayer, spoken from our knees as we knelt at her bed, was surely as simple and as pertinent as any He has heard. While theologians might have frowned, I felt God would have smiled when my daughter, who was hugging her favorite toy, added, "And Winnie-the-Pooh wants you to help my Mommy, too."

What amazed me that night—and, indeed, frequently took me by surprise in the nights and days to come—was my being able to find, or my being led, to places of inner peace. Much later, when speaking of this and of other experiences to a professional group, a psychologist intimated that I was protected from mental breakdown by either my denial of reality or by an extended state of shock. I could almost see the psychologist's lip curling when I spoke of a child's prayers for her mother's well-being.

Joe kept his word to Dr. Corbett. At seven the next morning I found myself in a small ward on the second floor of the neurology inpatient wing at the University of Iowa Hospital.

The receiving nurse would not allow me to wear my prettiest nightgown. For the spinal tap I was obliged to wear one of those cotton hospital gowns with ties at the back. Joe was tying the last one into a bow when a team of doctors and medical students walked in.

I was instructed to lie in the fetal position, my back to the white-coated company. The ties, so carefully done by Joe, were loosened. A female medical student, who blithely confessed that she had never undertaken the procedure before, was given the needle. Of course I couldn't see what was going on, but from the ribbing by other students and the running commentary, I gained a good picture of the scene behind me.

The nervous young woman jabbed my back three times before finding needle-entry to the spinal column. The draw-off of spinal fluid wasn't painful enough to evoke more than an ouch from me, but I didn't appreciate the students' banter. Had Joe been allowed to remain in the room I think a couple of the cruder students might have been in danger.

After the procedure was completed, the physician in charge gave me careful instructions to lie on my back for the next six hours. He told me that he didn't want me even to lift my head or wiggle a foot. So naturally I was puzzled when, a couple of hours later, a wheelchair was pushed into the ward and I was told that I was to be taken off for X rays.

To the radiologist who x-rayed me in positions that might have won a contortionist's nod of approval, I did make some mild reference to the instructions given earlier about my need to remain absolutely still. However, I don't think he listened to me as he clattered fresh film into the table slot or refocused his apparatus.

Without warning and while I was being wheeled back to my room, an excruciating headache hit me. I had never before had a headache that had not been exorcised by an aspirin. But the pain that now hit me caused me to cry out and to cradle my head against the slightest jar. Nurses and physicians were alerted. I felt relief when they injected a strong painkiller into a vein. Then I was aware that Dr. Corbett was in the room—others, too. Dr. Corbett was throwing out some angry questions. It was obvious that whoever it was—nurse, physician, or technician—who had permitted me to be taken to the X-ray lab was soon going to be facing his anger.

The headache, caused by my being moved too soon after a spinal tap, continued for forty-eight hours, but the pain was made bearable by strong painkillers—and by the arrival, first, of my parents and later, of Joe's parents. For the first days of my hospital stay one or another of my kin was with me for most of the daylight hours.

But I'm painting too bleak a picture, because for much of the time I was in the hospital I was given rich and loving support by family and friends.

I went through the whole gamut of emotions, and I thanked God for the shoulders that absorbed the tears. There were moments of laughter, too. I was, in fact, alone when one of the funniest incidents occurred.

Above my bed there was now a placard that read BLIND PATIENT in letters (so Joe had told me) about six inches tall. I'd had my supper when a hospital volunteer bustled into my ward. She was wheeling a cart that was in sore need of lubrication.

"Art cart! Art cart!" cried my visitor. I must have given her some expression of my confusion because she explained that she came around once a week to change the pictures on the walls of the different wards.

In a mid-Atlantic voice as hearty as a department store Santa Claus she continued, "I see you've got the Van Gogh irises. You like the French Impressionists, eh? Got a Monet here, or would you like a pretty English country scene? Think it's a Constable—you know, fields, trees, and a hay wagon. Yes, very peaceful."

Lowering her voice conspiratorially, she continued, "Some of those naughty men often ask me for a nude!" Her laughter rattled the cart. "I tell them no nudes. Does the wrong thing for their blood pressure!" The cart was again jiggled by giggles. "Of course, you can hang on to the Van Gogh if you want to and I'll . . . "

I guessed at what had caused her bright chatter to trail into a silence so heavy with embarrassment that it was almost tangible. She'd seen the sign above my bed.

The wheels of the art cart squeaked. From the door the volunteer murmured, "So sorry. Didn't realize. Tactless of me . . . So sorry . . . "

She also left me giggling. It was my first genuine laughter in far too long. It felt so good.

There was another unexpected visitor that evening. In the softest of Irish lilts, Mrs. O'Leary introduced herself. She was, she told me, the cleaning lady for this floor and she chose to work the evening shift.

"Gives me more time to make new friends, and 'sides, 'tis easier to use a mop in empty passages and elevators. And how are you, darlin', if you'll not mind me askin'?" She was speaking from the door and waiting, I assumed, to be invited in. I did so.

"I'd like to," she said, "but tonight I'm runnin' a tad late. There's a lad t'other side of the nurses' station needin' some hand-holdin'. But I will be seein' you. That I promise."

At our first encounter I had no inkling of how much Mrs. O'Leary's friendship would mean to me.

Shortly after this visit I was given the evening's third bonus—an unanticipated phone call.

"That you, Mom?" asked a childish voice which was certainly not Joy's. I was about to respond that the wrong number had been dialed when the voice said, "It's me, Jay."

My stepson had never called me Mom. His special name for me was Joannie. His mother lived quite close to Vinton.

"Oh, Jay! I'm so happy to hear you. Did your daddy tell you about me?"

"Yes, he told me your eyes are not seeing very well." His words were uttered so loudly that I was obliged to hold the phone three inches from my head. He provided an explanation for his shouting when he asked, "Do your ears work?"

"Oh, yes, they're fine," I reassured him.

With words now softly spoken Jay urged me to get well quickly. I promised I'd do my best and I asked him to thank his mother for helping him call me.

"Okay. Bye, Mom," said my seven-year-old stepson.

I held onto the receiver for quite a while as I reflected on how pleasing it was to hear a young boy calling me Mom. Jay already had a special place in my heart. He spent every second weekend in our home where he was hero-worshiped by Joy.

There were not many such happy moments, but they seemed to be given to me when I most needed them. I now find it hard to remember the sequence of my hospital experiences. I ran through a gauntlet of tests—magnetic resonance imaging, more X rays, many electroencephalographs, at least a dozen more visits to the cubicles where my eyes were examined through ophthalmoscopes, and twice that number of needles puncturing my arms to draw off blood for laboratory examination.

In one of my early physical examinations, a swollen lymph node was found in my right armpit. The doctors had seemed to be so excited about this discovery I had half expected them to shout "Eureka!"

However, I knew enough about medicine to understand that a swollen lymph node in this area of my body was not infrequently a sign of cancer. My stomach somersaulted and my mind spun through fresh tunnels of anxiety when I was told that a biopsy would be taken on the Wednesday of the following week.

"Why the delay?" I asked weakly.

The physician who had found the node flatly said that pathology was "all backed up." It was a thoughtless and not atypical dismissal of my obvious concern. I had six days to ponder the possibility of cancer.

On the Tuesday night before the biopsy was scheduled I was instructed to be ready by seven o'clock the next morning to go to the oncology department. An hour after dawn on the Wednesday I was washed, dressed, and had had coffee and toast. Seven o'clock came and went. So did eight o'clock, nine o'clock, ten o'clock. My anger came slowly to a boil, then steamed. Then I blew my lid.

A junior nurse who had been summoned by a slam on the call button got the full blast of my fury. A senior nurse was summoned and within five minutes, I was on a gurney being wheeled to an oncology room.

There, of course, I was smothered with apologies, but my anger evaporated only when the surgeon who examined my armpit said, "You may have had a swollen lymph node when you arrived at the hospital, Mrs. Beringer, but there's absolutely no sign of one now."

I could have kissed him then, but today I can still stimulate a spurt of anger by reflecting on how long I was kept, as Joe put it, "twisting in the wind."

In completing the story of the cancer scare I've moved ahead of the most critical day of my stay in the hospital.

Mom was with me when Dr. Corbett came to my room. Surprisingly, he was without any retinue—not even a nurse in attendance. I was unable to see his expression, of course, but by now I was becoming more sensitive to voice tone, even to body language, like the shuffling of feet or the cracking of a knuckle.

In fact, Dr. Corbett tweaked my toe. He had done that before. I presumed he saw this gesture as affectionate, tactile communication.

"And how is our Joan today?" he asked.

I was out of humorous or courteous responses. When I failed to reply he said, "You've been putting up with a lot, haven't you? We still don't have the answers. But it's time to tell you one thing."

"Yes?"

"All our tests, including the two spinal taps, have shown us that the deterioration in your eyesight is irreversible."

In the silence that followed, the word "irreversible" seemed to take on a life of its own. At its uttering, the word became a serpentine thing—twisting, humping, stretching, and, finally, coiling round my heart.

4

The Verdict

§

I've no recollection of how long that silence lasted after Dr. Corbett had told me, in effect, that I would be blind for the rest of my days. The next thing I recall is Mom squeezing my hand, and then how she rose from her chair and took a step toward the doctor.

She was in full control of her voice when she said, slowly, precisely, "Doctor, should you ever have to give another report like this to my daughter, I want you to be very sure that there is someone with her—someone who is close to her."

Although her words, uttered with such class, were not intended to be a rebuke, they struck a chord; there was genuine humility in the famous doctor's voice when he spoke again.

"Thank you, Mrs. Stuebbe, I promise to be sure of that." A pause and then, "It is not easy to be the bearer of bad news.

Unfortunately, in my work I often am. I do believe that it is best to be frank—at least with patients like your daughter who has . . . " (he felt for the phrase he wanted, and I liked it when he spoke it) . . . "an inner strength."

With maternal intuition, Mom knew what was now uppermost in my mind. She asked, "May my daughter go home now?"

Dr. Corbett cracked a knuckle. By now he certainly knew that I was quite numb, virtually paralyzed by his prognosis, for he spoke to Mom, not me.

He said, "Of course I understand how you, your daughter, and her family feel. A hospital is not a prison, so Joan has every right to go home. I hope she won't. Before she goes I'd like to taper down the heavy doses of steroids that we're now giving her. Her pleurisy and arthritis are responding. But my main reason for asking her to stay on in the hospital for some days is that our continuing research of her case and some more tests may well prove helpful, perhaps sight-saving, to others who may be stricken down as she's been stricken."

Mom asked guardedly, "What do you mean by research, doctor? My daughter is not a laboratory animal."

Dr. Corbett said, "I fear I've not made it clear how unique and important your daughter's case study is. We're in touch with ophthalmologists, neurologists, virologists, and other specialists in other hospitals. We're tied into a network of physicians and scientists from Boston to Florida to California. I don't want to get into the technical language. I'm sure you don't want me to talk about autoimmune retinopathy or pathologic proteins. There'll be time to explain what we're finding. The foe that hit Joan's eyes was fast, furious, ruthless, and, speaking for the enemy, effective. It was like an attack from kamikaze pilots. We know you have macular degeneration—normally a malady of aging—but we don't know what caused it. If we can identify the foe we may be able to set up a defense system that could save the sight of others."

Mom was still my champion and spokesperson. "How long do you want to keep her?" she asked.

The doctor said, "A week, perhaps, ten days, maybe."

Mom grasped my hand once more. "What do you say, Joan?" she asked.

"Yes, Joan, it is, of course, up to you," said Dr. Corbett.

I licked dry lips. I was already wondering how Joe was going to cope with a blind wife—could I cook for him, clean house, do the laundry, do the shopping? And what about my three-year-old? Could I, as a blind mother, lead her through childhood to womanhood?

I became aware of another long silence. Oh, yes, they had asked me if I would stay in the hospital—not for my sake alone. For the very first time I was given the thought that I could be helpful to others. It was a good thought.

I nodded. "Yes, I'll stay," I whispered.

"Thank you, Joan," said Dr. Corbett. "You're a brave young woman."

I thought, *Oh why do you have to say things like that? I'm not brave at all. I'm scared, so terribly scared.*

When the doctor had left the room Mom pressed her cheek to mine. In her comforting me I felt that I was myself a child again. How many times had I run to her with a grazed knee or when distraught from a brother's teasing. Now I sobbed, "I'm blind! Mom, I'm blind! I'll always be blind!"

I remember one phrase in my mother's efforts to soften my sorrow. She said, "But you're the most beautiful blind girl in the world." I would have protested her perhaps maudlin remarks had I not received them as a child. She spoke the Lord's Prayer, too, and, when my throat permitted, I joined her in some phrases—"Thy will be done . . . Deliver us from evil . . . "

I was so grateful (I still am) that my mother was there to see me through the first shock of understanding that I would not see again—not my daughter's sweet face, not daffodils or tulips, not an avenue of trees in springtime, not a work of art, not a ballerina's pirouette—not a movie, not a baseball game, not, not, not . . .

But there were others who did not know the prognosis and who were entitled to know it as soon as possible. After Mom had fluffed my pillows and when my sobbing had stopped, I asked her to phone the Braille School and ask Joe to come as soon as possible.

"He must bring Joy, too. I need to see them both. I want to see them separately," I said. "Don't tell Joe anything more than that he is needed. I want to tell them in my own way."

Mom gave her promise and, sensibly or tactfully, said that she would phone Vinton from the hospital lobby.

So I was quite alone for perhaps half an hour, and glad to be so, before my favorite nurse, Katy, looked in on me. She was petite, always upbeat, a brunette (she told me so); we had shared a lot. She had accompanied me to many of my tests and she had volunteered to read the letters and cards that were coming in from all over.

I was so pleased to have letters (phone calls, too) from my brothers who, in recent years, had not been more than Christmas-card close to me. Katy had difficulty reading some of the letters, especially those painstakingly written by the partially sighted kids at the Braille School. When she choked up, I choked up, too. Then both of us would laugh—quality laughter that accompanies tears of gratitude.

Katy and I had a number of common interests and experiences. She, for instance, like Joe, had married a high school sweetheart. Also like Joe, she had found teenage love to be immature. Like Joe's, her first marriage had broken up. Although Katy was my junior by eighteen months, she had also had a daughter only a year older than Joy.

"Just checking you out," said Katy from the door of my room. "By the way, I do know the bad news. Dr. Corbett told us. I am so sorry."

"Please, Katy," I pleaded, "don't say any more at the moment. I want to look okay for my husband, who'll be here soon."

"Understood," said Katy. "But if your guy's on his way I'd better give your hair a brush."

"Is it that bad?"

"Not if he likes haystacks," she said, and we both laughed and hugged.

She stood back to admire her handiwork, hummed approval, and then confessed to having left one loose hair across the bridge of my nose and cheek.

"You remind me of my Heidelberg catechism," I told her.

"Sounds heavy," said Katy, now plucking the hair from my face. "There! Got it!" she exclaimed.

"The response to question one in my catechism," I told her, "was 'without the will of the Father, not a hair can fall from your head.'"

"That right?" exclaimed my favorite but agnostic nurse. "Sounds neat! From way back in Sunday school I seem to remember about sparrows falling from trees and the counting of hairs. Well, if it's true, God's recount will show that you've got one hair less than you had a minute ago."

There was no mockery in her renewed laughter. She kissed my forehead, made for the door, and said, "It's okay, Joan, I'm not going to say anything to make you cry, but I just want to say that if you stay here much longer you'll make a believer of me once again."

I told her that she couldn't have paid me a nicer compliment. She chuckled and was gone.

Thanks in part to Katy, I really was ready for Joe when he arrived at six o'clock. I sensed his surprise at finding me composed and well-groomed. I guessed he had wheedled something out of Mom because, after kissing me, he said, "News not so good, huh? Your mother said that you wanted to see Joy and me separately. Right?"

"Right," I said and then I went on to tell him Dr. Corbett's prognosis. He was sitting on the bed, and when I used the word "irreversible" he jumped to his feet.

"I'm not going to believe that," he said. "Nor must you. Never did like that Dr. Corbett. I know he doesn't like me either. What right has he to say that 'you're permanently blind'?"

I helped him along. "Joe, we've got to come to terms with the facts. I'm terribly, terribly sorry. What hurts me most, what makes my heart ache, is that I'm going to be a burden to you."

I could tell he had been speaking from the window, his face turned away from me. I tried in vain to picture his expression. Was it anger, fear, frustration, disbelief, or horror? In a moment I had the answer. He turned around, then pushed me to one side of the bed so that he could lie on the other. Then he cradled my head. Although he did not make a sound, I could tell from the jerkiness of his breathing that he was trying to keep his crying under control.

It was strange, but I now found myself doing the comforting. I stroked his face, thanked him for his courage and care.

After a while he made an attempt at a joke. He said something about a hospital bed being less comfortable than a rocky campground.

When I suggested that it was time for me to see Joy, he agreed, but told me that he was going to spend the night with me.

"It's okay," he said with forced laughter. "I'm going to sleep right here on the floor."

It was not the appropriate moment to speak about hospital rules.

A couple of minutes later Joy arrived and came hesitantly to my open arms. Joe and Mom left us alone. It was harder now to keep my resolve to hold back the tears. Joy was lying on my tummy, her breath soft against my neck, when I told her, "Honey, I wanted you here with me—just the two of us—so that I could tell you something that's important to both of us. I think you knew that I wasn't seeing well. That was why I had to stop driving and why I couldn't read to you. But now I have to tell you that my eyes are not working at all."

I'd planned to give her a long silence so that she could digest what I'd told her, but Joy responded at once and with a generous offer.

With sweet solemnity she asked, "Mommy, can I kiss your eyes better?"

I gave her a hug, and tears were under my eyelids. "Whenever you kiss me, I always feel better," I assured her.

Joy wriggled up over my body a few inches higher and planted butterfly kisses on my eyelids.

A moment, then, "Mommy, why do your eyes taste salty?" From my throat came an uncontrollable cry of pain. Alarmed, Joy pulled away from me, arching her back. Breathlessly she asked, "Oh, Mommy, did I hurt your broken eyes?"

After a moment or two of holding her to my breast, I was able to say, "Honey, sometimes people cry not because they've been hurt but because their hearts are overflowing with love."

She pondered this for some seconds, then asked, "Mommy, do hearts make tears?"

"The most beautiful ones of all," I assured her.

Another thoughtful pause in which I could almost hear her mind reaching for new concepts. "Mommy, I'm glad your broken eyes can still make beautiful tears."

I bent my lips to her forehead and wept quite unashamedly into the silk of my daughter's hair.

The gold and glory of our lives is surely created by such moments—moments that put no stress on memory, for they are stored in the most secure caches of our minds or, as I prefer it, within the secret and most sacred chambers of our hearts.

I've known and talked with those who have been born blind, among them many of the blind children given to my care, and I've come to believe that imagination is more important to them than memory. Speak to them of color, for instance, and they will often relate color to the sense of touch or sound. Red is likely, within their thinking, to have a harsh texture, but green or blue may "feel" as soft as silk or perhaps be related to the clear, sweet sound of a flute.

But those, like me, who have lost their sight in later years draw constantly upon memory. My daughter is now in her teenage years, and while I have not been able to see the maturing of her face and figure, memory allows me still to look into her dark brown eyes and see the sparkle in them when she's amused, see their widening in wonder on her discovering something new or observing something that delights her.

I cannot conceive that anyone values memory more than I. Thank heavens, too, for a good forgettery. Perhaps the most important attributes of pain and sorrow are their abilities to fade, to self-blunt, as it were, to lose those sharp, serrated edges which rip a heart.

So those long days in the hospital and the longer nights have so melded now that I'm obliged to probe and pry out the incidents that might hold interest. Joe did, in fact, sleep on the floor in my room that night after I'd told him of the permanency of my loss of vision. I suspect that the nursing staff had been advised—possibly by Dr. Corbett—to pretend they had not seen or heard the snoring figure in the corner.

But there was one midnight visitor. Mrs. O'Leary, the buxom cleaning lady, called in, and was so amused to find Joe with me that she had difficulty stifling her laughter. Her concern was not that hospital rules had been defied but was only for Joe's comfort. From an empty room next door she brought a pillow and a blanket, and so gentle was she in covering him and placing the pillow under his head that Joe's snoring was not interrupted by a quaver.

When he was awakened by the sound of the breakfast cart, Joe expressed guilt that he had slept so well. Leaving the telltale pillow and blanket on the floor, he crept out of the room and returned to Vinton. I did not tell Joe that on that night—and, indeed, through almost all my nights in the hospital—I slept for less than two hours.

Many, perhaps most, hospital patients discover that at night, and especially in the small hours, the swing of a clock's pendulum slows down, and there are many more than sixty minutes to the hour. I began to dread the nighttime, the introspective hours when, to the sleepless, the imps of anxiety become brooding ogres.

The solution to the problem of my restless, fitful, and totally unprofitable hours came from an unexpected quarter. I was listening to a radio program when a talk-show host interviewed a former Vietnam prisoner of war who had survived four years of solitary confinement. He related how his plane had been shot down, how he had been captured and tortured before being isolated in a prison cell.

Asked how he had managed to avoid going crazy under such

conditions, the veteran replied that he had compiled an autobiography.

"Of course, I had neither pen nor writing paper," he related. "But in my head I recalled the events of my life, and, where memory served me well, in minutest detail. I climbed familiar trees again, walked my neighbor's fences, re-created conversations with siblings, cousins, classmates, the coach of my football team, whoever . . . By the time my solitary confinement ended, my life story would have competed in volume length with *The Encyclopaedia Britannica . . .*"

I was more than intrigued, I was fascinated by the former POW's self-designed therapy, which had saved his sanity. By chance, I was listening to this radio program shortly after my second spinal tap. This time I was taking very seriously the instructions to lie absolutely still for six hours.

While I wasn't being tortured—not maliciously anyway—and while a touch of the call button on the nightstand would bring another human being to my side, there were times when I felt my sanity was threatened.

Since I did not want to be carted off to the hospital's psychiatric wing, I would be careful not to voice my story aloud. But my lips certainly moved, and a sensitive microphone might well have picked up my whisper when, with some excitement, I began to compile my story.

"Once upon a time," I started in the manner and tradition of every good story of early childhood, "yes, once upon a time—actually in California at seven in the evening of January 22, 1952—a baby girl was born to Vivian, the wife of the Reverend Robert Stuebbe. They christened her Joan. And then . . . "

5

A Serpentless Eden

❦

When the bustle and business of the great hospital had quietened and sleep had forsaken me, remembrances of my childhood and young adult years not only kept depression at bay but often, as I lost myself in livelier scenes or situations, I felt quite exhilarated.

In reliving my life story I was not at all disciplined and often ignored chronology. Memory behaved like a sprightly gazelle, leaping from intended routes and hard pavements, as it were, to graze a while in sun-speckled glens.

One phenomenon that may well be explained by the newness of my loss of vision is that the different scenes re-created from memory were so vivid, so highly colored. I wondered if blindness had one modest compensation—the brightening and sharpening of the images thrown upon the screen of my mind.

Since I had little if any recollection of my first three years of life, the first slide I inserted into the projector of memory was of a sunbaked California playground. I am five. My towheaded friend, Kip (I can see his red pants and yellow shirt), has put a beetle (a lizard? a caterpillar?) down my blouse. I feel the critter squirming against my tummy.

I am so disgusted, so incensed, that with all the strength of a skinny arm I punch Kip on his freckled nose. Down he goes—howling. Another child shouts to an authority figure that Joan has just killed Kip. Horror grips me. But if Kip is dead, why is he still kicking his legs like that?

Of course, Kip made a rapid recovery and we became friends again. But it was close to the time of this playground incident that I had my first encounter with death. On the road outside our parsonage home I found a cat that had recently been run over. In stroking the fur my hand had been smeared with warm blood.

Dad had tried to explain to a dismayed child that all living things, even people, died.

Most of us, I now reflected as this slide of remembrance faded, could recall their trauma and confusion on first discovering that life was close-margined by death, and that even beautiful things like tabby cats died. What about fathers and mothers? I had asked. Surely fathers couldn't possibly die! How hard it is for adults to enter the minds of young children attempting to probe life's mysteries.

Insofar as I could recall, my childhood was lived out in a serpentless Eden.

I had—and still gratefully have—two brothers. Bob is seven years my senior and Jon five years older than I am. These age spans were wide enough in childhood to be a barrier against demonstrative or close fraternal affection.

I was gratefully aware that they were not among those who were scooped into the bloodied paddy fields of Vietnam. At the time, Bob was on special assignment at Camp David, where he worked in some capacity for President Johnson. Today he works in one of the higher echelons of national defense. Jon spent a year at the Air Force Academy in Colorado before deciding that flying supersonic jets was not his premier ambition. He went on to become a lawyer and, today, he is a California judge.

Indisputably, my early childhood's closest friend was four-legged and fictional. Even in my most tender conscious years my imagination thrived. I could at any time enter a world of fantasy outmatching anything in the *Arabian Nights*.

Stabled within my mind was Princess, a fleet-footed, golden palomino mare that could gallop me along white-surfed beaches to distant continents or around the sawdust of a three-ringed circus. I was never more content, even into my eleventh year, than when riding—barebacked, of course, my hair streaming—that surefooted imaginary mare with a silver-white mane.

I mounted her, let me now confess, during catechism classes or when forced to accompany a more tiresome parishioner on a Sunday afternoon walk.

Princess imbued me with a passion for riding that I have not relinquished. Watch the expression of a sightless person when he or she is mounted on a horse and there'll be some comprehension of their sense of liberation.

As I lay wide awake at three o'clock one morning I relived another fabulous ride. This time my mount was as real as rain (Princess had long ago taken her final gallop over a horizon of fantasy), and I was a nineteen-year-old college student in South Dakota.

The horse, a high-spirited gelding named Midnight, was

owned by one of my father's parishioners who had generously invited me to exercise him whenever I had the time or felt the inclination. Dad's ministry then was in the little town of Menno, not far from the University of South Dakota.

On this particular ride I headed Midnight into what I've heard South Dakotans refer to as Nowhere Land—those stretches of countryside where, so often, no habitation can be seen.

I cannot recall what it was that day that created such a close harmony of nature—the trees (not many in this countryside), the sweep and gentle fold of fields, the sky with its blues shifting from soft hues where they touched the earth, to deep azure in the dome above. The timpanic beat of Midnight's hooves, a-trot, mostly, a-gallop in short spurts, added rhythm to the music and the poetry of the hour. The solitude was no less than spiritual.

Then, suddenly and unexpectedly, over the next rise I saw a dwelling, an isolated farmhouse which, as I approached it, was obviously abandoned, vacant, its windows broken, its paintwork peeling and discolored. The montage—the grass all about rippling in the gentle breeze, a warped fence that must at one time have enclosed a garden, for there were flowers blooming among the weeds—recalled an Andrew Wyeth painting. If others had been riding with me they might have described the house as spooky, but for me it blended marvelously with an enchanted landscape.

I tied Midnight to a rusty hand pump and, without a thought of trespassing or of danger, I entered and explored the forlorn building. Boards groaned underfoot, and the only piece of furniture was a broken kitchen chair. A few strips of torn and faded cloth hung across north-facing windows.

Then, as I sat cross-legged on a crumbling porch that gave a wide vista of the prairie, I tried to people the house as it once had been. I seemed to hear the laughter of young children, the splash of water in a bucket under the pump where Midnight was now straining for a more succulent patch of clover.

The breeze carried to me the scents of wild herbs, the acrid but not unpleasant smell of Midnight's sweating hide. Yet I picked up, too, or so it seemed, the delectable smell of fresh bread just taken from the kitchen oven. I heard (I felt so sure I did), above the birdsong, the sweep of a long skirt such as was worn at the beginning of the century. It had to have been the skirt of the former mistress of this now derelict abode.

So deeply engraved was this memory, abstracted from the last year of my teens, that, even lying in a hospital bed with almost totally sightless eyes, I could re-create it in all dimensions; in so doing, what would have been a restless, troubled hour was shortened and wonderfully sweetened.

The nurse on duty walked softly to my bedside.

"Still awake?" she asked.

I was quite startled by the interruption, and a tad resentful, too.

"Yes," I told the nurse, "I'm quite okay."

"Want me to give you something to help you sleep?" she asked.

"No, I really don't," I responded in the manner of a young child just distracted from play.

In urging me to try to sleep, the nurse reminded me that I would be undergoing a number of new tests in the morning. When she had left the room, I attempted to recapture the peace and the beauty of that memorable ride into Nowhere Land. I managed one more fleeting glimpse. I saw myself riding away from the abandoned house. I heard myself resolving that one day I would return.

I never did. I never will.

On the next night in the hospital the duty nurse again tried to talk me into taking some sleeping pill. I think she would have persuaded me to swallow it had I not by now become so very intrigued by trying to relive my earlier years. I again acknowledged that, as a biographer, I had not been doing too well. I had not, for instance, given any description of my parents. Nor had I related how I came to be working with blind children.

Dad came from stolid Dutch-German stock. On first encounter, a stranger might have seen an austere man, too serious perhaps, a man who had difficulty showing or expressing his emotions. In fact, his whole life as a minister of the Reformed Church of the United States, one of the smaller Calvinist denominations, was dedicated to the well-being of his fellow men, to their spiritual growth, of course, but also to helping his parishioners—indeed, people of all faith and of no faith at all—to find solutions to personal problems ranging from domestic strife and economic hardship to illness and grief.

A cameo that comes to mind, one that may give firmer substance to my father's flesh and faith, is of his sitting for four hours through a wintry afternoon with a suicidal mother on the gravestone of her child.

The child had accidentally drowned and the mother had held herself responsible. I had watched Dad persuading the distraught woman that life still held meaning, and that her child had been received into the gentlest of all arms. My father had instructed my brother Jon to circle the cemetery frequently in the family's car in the event that medical, as well as spiritual, help was needed. I had been with Jon.

I have no remembrance of my father ever having punished me, but I can still quiver when recollecting the look that he could give me if he ever felt I had strayed from what he considered appropriate conduct.

There was one such typical reprimand in my young childhood. I had invited a group of classmates to my home, which
was alongside the church. The concrete areas around the buildings were well suited to roller-skating. After we had spun our
wheels around the church for about an hour, one of my friends
suggested we play a game of hide-and-seek. The church, with its
crannies, pews, and organ loft were ideal for this game, and I
knew where my father kept the key.

Soon the sanctified building was filled with the squeals of
children at play. From his adjacent office Dad must have heard us.
He found me hiding in the pulpit. His eyes bored into my own
like lasers. He never said a word to me about the incident. He
didn't have to!

I found my Christian faith because both Mom and Dad lived
it—I was constantly exposed to the problems encountered by
Dad's flock and to the care that was needed and so readily given.
Christ's commandments—to love God and neighbor with all our
hearts—became as essential to my well-being as breathing in and
breathing out.

How to describe Mom? I suppose I gained my bearing from
her. I see her as elegantly graceful. I'm sure the genes she
bequeathed to me account for the airier side of my nature. She
once laughingly told me that I had run and danced before I had
walked, and that I had laughed before I'd learned to cry.

Perhaps if Mom had not been a preacher's wife she could
have been a part-time model, a part-time teacher, a part-time
counselor, a part-time seamstress. For me, she embraced all the
exemplary virtues—she still does. Speaking pastorally, she was
always in the background, but I believe the eyes of those who
saw my parents together would frequently shift from the
preacher to the woman who supported him. In doing so they

would better understand the conviction and strength of the man.

In any event, and in grateful tribute to my parents, I can say that I grew up in a happy and marvelously secure environment. I learned, too, that there's a sharply defined line between right and wrong.

While I lay in my hospital bed I shifted from tears to laughter and back again to tears with what, in less traumatic circumstances, might have been regarded as unstable frequency. Favorite Nurse Kate was taken aback when I exploded into tears as she read me a letter from my closest childhood friend, Louise . . . Louise, with her fiery Basque blood, and I had once been inseparable. However, we had lost touch in recent years. But she had heard through the Bakersfield grapevine about my loss of sight. In her letter she told me she was ready immediately to fly to my bedside. Her sympathy, her love, the image of her darkly beautiful and animated face just tore me apart.

However, I was back on an even keel again when Katy asked me how the "autobiography" was going.

"It'll need a lot of editing," I told her. "Louise alone deserves a full chapter. Maybe I'll give her one later on."

Katy, who now said she could spare me no more time without being fired, urged me to "keep at it—because the therapy is obviously doing you a power of good."

Perhaps this was true. In those first days and weeks of knowing that I would never see again, I could believe that my sanity was protected, in part, anyway, by this unusual and often quite demanding occupation first suggested to me by an unknown Vietnam POW.

On the following night when I was sleepless I found myself thinking of my senior year in high school.

It was a good year, and one not entirely unimportant reason for declaring it to be so was because, at last, I was filling out my sweater. At the age of fifteen I had reached my full height of five foot nine inches, yet I weighed only ninety-five pounds! Louise had charitably called me willowy, but more than a couple of guys had nicknamed me Twiggy, a name once elevated in the world of high fashion, but which, in the classroom, embarrassed me acutely.

I had had no intention of becoming a professional model (although the idea had been suggested), but I did entertain the notion of becoming a professional dancer. I was not thinking so much of the second line of the chorus at Las Vegas as I was of being a dance teacher. I particularly enjoyed modern dance and I had, my teacher told me, been blessed with some talent; but I was constantly pulled toward a career that would be less self-serving.

In any event, in my senior year, when I was eyeing boys (and, I was pleased to note, when boys were now eyeing me) the idea of working with and for people who had special needs became more sharply focused.

My father's decision to accept a ministry in South Dakota was to prove critical to my own life. My parents had lived in California since before I was born. I had not thought of myself as a typical Californian, but this is how I was regarded when, with long blonde hair, a golden tan, and stereotypically long legs, I entered the University of South Dakota in Vermillion.

For my parents, traveling to the Midwest was, as they themselves put it, "going home." They had been married in Wisconsin and Dad had gone to school in South Dakota. For me it was a foreign land, but a land that I quickly learned to love. Certainly I was shocked by the winter weather. I, who had spent about eleven months of the year in shorts and T-shirts, now had to invest in long johns, padded snowsuits, thick mittens, and ear-muffs to face conditions that I had seen only in movies about Eskimos and wolves.

I had never seen snow falling; snow to me was something that sparkled only on distant peaks. An unforgettable memory is of my first crunching walk over virgin snow that street lights had turned into a pathway of diamonds.

It was not only the beauty of winter that I loved, but the indescribable wonder of the spring and fall. In this, the heartland of America, the people were so different, too—so welcoming, hospitable, people still true to the creeds and aspirations of the founding fathers. Surely Norman Rockwell found much inspira-tion in this country where mothers were still honored, flags were flown bravely and high, and every kitchen seemed to smell of apple pie.

My friends in California had warned me that in the Dakotas the mail was still delivered by the pony express. I felt sorry for those in the Golden State who had had no experience of the warmth of South Dakota's hearths.

All too quickly, it had seemed to me, I had graduated from the University of South Dakota with the credentials to practice as a recreational therapist. What I did not anticipate was that my first jobs would be at the Yankton mental institution and the women's correctional facility—a euphemism for a grim, gray-stoned jail—which were sited in the same well-guarded grounds.

Immediately assigned work in both institutions, I was instructed to program and plan leisure activities. Several of my "clients" (as they were always designated) had been incarcerated for homicide. On my first day on the job I was introduced to a dozen clients, the majority of them weighing at least two hundred pounds, and the heaviest having ax-murdered her unfaithful spouse.

A colleague laughingly told me later that on my first day of work I had reminded him of a prairie dog caught in the headlights of a truck—rigid from alarm, paws defensively raised, and eyes like Frisbees! At the end of each working day there was no sweeter sound than the clanging of a steel door behind me, me being on the same side as the keys!

Sometimes I was put in charge of more docile groups, a few even younger than my twenty-two years. Several had fried their brains with drugs. To me they were more tragic than those who, while insane, had committed heinous crimes.

There were new and often alarming experiences every day. In the gym one day I was naive enough to toss a twenty-pound medicine ball to a woman who could have been a professional wrestler. The first time she tossed it back the ball slipped through my hands and hit my chest with a sound like a bass drum. On regaining my breath I rolled the ball back to her. This was a mistake! The woman's second throw bounced me into the wall of the gymnasium, which then echoed with maniacal laughter. I persuaded her to change the game to Ping-Pong.

A much more serious incident occurred on an institution bus in which we took quieter clients for trips into the country. I was the allocated driver on the day that Dolly, a psychotic, was given her first outing in months. She had been, I was assured, quite docile in recent weeks. However, the adventure of the outing proved to be too much for Dolly. We had just gotten underway when Dolly seized a huge fistful of my hair and started to drag me back over the driver's seat. My hands were unable to reach the steering wheel, my feet unable to touch the pedals, and my neck seemed to be within an inch of fracture.

Two assistants aboard rushed to my rescue and managed to subdue Dolly. The bus, which had left the road, stalled only one yard from the trunk of a huge oak tree. My scalp hurt for a month. It was a close call.

At the end of each workday, my colleagues and I felt we had not only earned our modest salaries, but also our right to relax and enjoy ourselves. Along with several others who held professional jobs at the Yankton prison or the mental institution (or, as in my case, at both), I lived in The Alley, a row of houses so small that they might have been constructed for dwarves.

We enjoyed a communal spirit, and perhaps one reason for my own popularity was that my large and ancient Ford (the odometer had broken down at 145,000 miles) was sometimes the only vehicle on The Alley to start up when the thermometer was below zero! It was also the only car that seemed capable of plowing its way through two feet of snow—even with a dozen of us aboard!

"And what about your love life?" asked Nurse Katy who, when time permitted, had been catching up on the "autobiography."

I raised my eyebrows (a gesture she may not have observed). "Love life?"

"Don't play the innocent with me," said Katy (smiling, I'm sure) as she tucked in the bedsheets. "When a golden-tanned California blonde drops out of the sky onto a South Dakota campus, the guys must have thought they'd joined Alice in Wonderland."

"Oh, sure," I told her, "there were two or three guys whose company I enjoyed a lot, and one I shared poetry with."

"Only poetry?"

"You're far too inquisitive," I told my favorite nurse and now my friend. "Besides, that was a long time ago."

Katy clicked a skeptical tongue, sat on the end of the bed, and asked about Joe.

"Oh, he was much later," I said. "I'd first known him in college when he'd been married to his high school sweetheart. Like me, he graduated as a recreational therapist. Eventually, he found the job he wanted at the Braille School in Vinton."

I went on to tell Katy how, after Joe's divorce, I had met up with him again when he drove once or twice a month to Vermillion, half an hour's drive from Yankton, to see his baby son whom he adored. At first, I had admired Joe's dedication to his work. Then we had had a few dates and watched football and baseball games together. Then we realized that we had fallen in love.

"As simple as that?" asked Katy.

"Almost as simple as that," I replied. "But where are the parents of an only daughter who are ready to uncork champagne when she shows them an engagement ring given by a man they've never met?"

Katy surprised me by saying, "I only wish my parents had cared enough to worry about my engagement. If they'd done so, I might have had second thoughts myself and . . . heck, there's been a lot of water under the bridge since that awful scene."

I reached out a hand to her. "Was it that bad?"

A deep sigh. "Worse," she said. "We got married in Vegas, and then my Johnny Ex blew half our honeymoon funds in Caesar's Palace. He drowned his grief and my screams of rage in bourbon. As Shakespeare so succinctly put it, 'What fools these brunettes be!'"

"Shakespeare?" I queried.

"Well, substitute 'these mortals' for the brunettes and you've got Puck's exact quote out of *A Midsummer Night's Dream*."

"You're so full of surprises," I told her.

"Oh, sure," she replied. "Can you forget the lines you spoke in a convent school play?" She obviously looked at her watch, for she gasped and said, "Is that really the time! Mrs. Whatshername must still be on a bedpan."

She left me laughing so hard that my stomach hurt.

I was obliged to postpone telling Katy how my parents had soon come around to accepting Joe and how in the summer of 1978 Dad had married us in Manitowoc, Wisconsin, where he had taken up a new (and his last) ministry.

In the course of Dad's message to us he said, "I only wish I could promise you a stormless voyage as you, Joe, and you, my Joan, set out together. But that I cannot do, because only God knows what lies ahead for us. What I can promise is that if you seek God's navigation for your lives you'll be able to face whatever storms you might encounter . . . "

Now, as I recall and record the words Dad spoke on that carefree day when I married Joe, I find myself foolishly wondering whether we would have been too daunted to make our solemn vows had we but glimpsed the perils and pain that lay ahead for both of us.

6

An Angel Unawares

§

Mimicking an Indian love call, Nurse Katy burst through the door of my room. "Big Chief Bald Eagle's on his way," she announced, "and I'm just checking to see you don't have spinach on your earlobes!"

"Do you mind translating?" I requested. It was a plea I frequently made to Katy, who had a talent for making mundane duties and other things sound complex or hilarious.

She removed my lunch tray and then explained that Dr. Corbett himself and an Indian guy from the Mayo Clinic ("or somewhere") were on their way—the nurses' station had just been informed of the VIP visitors. She added, "And by the way, there's no spinach on your teeth or your earlobes." We both giggled. Katy's visits to my ward were always refreshing.

"What's the Mayo man like?" I asked.

"Young enough," she responded, "possibly eligible, wearing a turban. Anyway, I'm not sure I want to live in Pakistan or wherever." Another giggle was curtailed when Dr. Corbett and the Indian physician entered.

Dr. Corbett greeted me with his usual toe-tweaking. He said, "Good news for you, Joan." I held my smile because I had heard him disappointingly utter this phrase before. In the pause that followed I presumed he was reading my chart. The only "good news" I was ready to accept at this point was for him to tell me that his prognosis had been horribly wrong and that my eyes would soon be on the mend.

He didn't tell me this, of course. I was now only too well aware that the prognosis was grimly correct. I knew that my sight was limited to the smallest aperture of peripheral vision which, in certain conditions, allowed me to distinguish light from dark and the vaguest of shapes and movements.

What Dr. Corbett did say, almost jovially, was, "Well, Joan, tomorrow you're going home!"

In the word "home" there was music, and I believe it was to that music that I immediately responded. I felt a surge of blood flush my cheeks.

Yet all too quickly the music became a screech of alarm.

I realized that this small room in this huge hospital had protected me from the real world, a world created for people with vision; a mobile world of automobiles, trains, planes, elevators, and even supermarket carts; a world in which south for me could as well be north, east as well be west.

In theory I'd known about this visionless world that I must now face. For five years I'd made a career of helping a hundred and more children cope with the most basic demands of living, like the simple task of laying toothpaste along the bristles of a brush.

But from tomorrow it would be I who would be blindly feeling my way beyond the walls and safety of this room. I'd be having to put my own toothpaste on my own brush. I'd be having to spread invisible peanut butter on a slice of invisible bread. I would be having sightlessly to provision my home, to dust, to clean . . .

As this scary thinking ran amok, Dr. Corbett must have observed the sudden change in my expression. He misunderstood my tightened jaw, or perhaps my sudden clutching of the sheets. His voice was kind, almost sorrowful, as he said, "How we wish we could have done more for you, Joan. Perhaps one day, perhaps within your lifetime, though doubtfully within mine, we may learn how to replace dead optical nerves with receptors that will respond to light and transmit signals to the brain."

As he spoke to me from the foot of the bed, I acknowledged that I liked this man who had given to my case all his accumulated skill and the wisdom of his long experience. I wanted to thank him for his efforts to help me, but I didn't trust my voice. I nodded, though, when he asked if the visiting Pakistani physician might examine my eyes with a handheld ophthalmoscope.

After this brief examination (was it now a hundred times they'd scanned my eyes through instruments?), the two men held a brief conference. Then Dr. Corbett addressed me again.

He said, "What we are trying to do, Joan, is to sequence out the pathological proteins in your case. You'd be surprised at the length of your clinical and laboratory history. My colleagues and I—and I include specialists in hospitals across the country—believe you've been the victim of a lupuslike ailment."

He went on to explain that, for reasons not yet understood, women in their third decade were the most vulnerable to lupus, and that I fell into the "vulnerable bracket." He emphasized that they were not labeling my malady lupus, but that "kinship to lupus had been observed."

Before he left, Dr. Corbett pleaded with me to make regular outpatient visits to the hospital to help in the continuing study of my case. He assured me once again that I had been "a most cooperative and courageous patient." Then, in an avuncular tone, he added, "And the prettiest patient I've seen for a very long time!" Sensing that he was about to give a valedictory tweak to my big toe I protectively hugged my knees.

Then I began to think about going home.

The word "home" (be it spoken in any language) is, I suppose, among the richest in our vocabulary, and for most folks it conjures up so much more than furnishings or the materials from which it is constructed.

Our home was certainly much more than merely a white clapboard house (circa 1950) made affordable by being within train-whistle distance of the railroad tracks. The house itself was able to keep out all but the prairie's most bitter blasts of winter and all but the most stifling heat of summer. It had become our castle, albeit modest, and no matter the season, when Joe, Joy, and I were inside and we had, as it were, pulled up the draw-bridge, we felt removed for a spell from the cruelties, the ugliness, the pain and perils of the world. We had clung to the erroneous belief that when we were at home nothing could threaten us, nothing could disturb or hinder our smooth, contented, and rewarding journey into the fresh decades.

In some ways the last but one day of my hospital stay was my worst. Certainly there had been days of pain and grieving for my lost sight, but most of the time I had been marvelously supported by the love and care of family and friends.

But for one reason or another I had no visitors on that last afternoon or in the evening, either. Perhaps this was one reason for my thoughts focusing on such chilling questions.

At the Braille School I'd become skilled in teaching sightless others the daily living skills. How many had I shown how to use the sensitive skin on the back of the hand to pour salt from a shaker into a bowl of soup or stew. How many had I shown how to use a cane to move around furniture, to walk a street, to find one's way across a campus. How many had I shown how to arrange clothes in a closet for their easy choosing.

But could the teacher now teach herself?

I was ashamed that I'd seen my hospital ward as a sort of security blanket. Yet I was unable to put aside the thought that I had survived these past weeks because there were people at my beck and call, and that my every need was met. Even eating had been made simple. At mealtimes there was an aide or orderly there to bone the chicken or to cut steak into small, chewable pieces.

Joe was at his office when I phoned with the news that I would be ready to be picked up at ten the following morning. There was obviously somebody with him, because his response was crisp and businesslike. A neighbor would baby-sit for Joy and he would come alone.

I was tempted to call Mom and Dad to ask them if they could manage to drive to Vinton once again and help lead me gently into a new lifestyle, a new world. But before it became too seductive, I put this temptation behind me.

I believe I spoke aloud to an empty room—and, if I did so, it was through gritted teeth—when I declared, "No, I'm going to do it myself! Blind as I am, I'm going to be a good wife and a good mother and perhaps a good teacher still." The help I would most need would be God's alone to give.

The hours following Dr. Corbett's visit were among the strangest and most stressful of my stay in the hospital. Following moments of high resolve, I would have spells of such turmoil that I would thump my temples with my palms. I asked myself if I was going crazy—as crazy as some of those women at the Yankton mental institution, women who had lost touch with reality.

It was within the span of one of my worst spells that Katy looked in on me. Her joke died on her lips as she marked my distress.

"Oh, Joan," she exclaimed, "what's the matter? . . . I'd expected you to be elated by the news of your going home."

I turned my face into the pillow and began to sob. "I'm so scared, Katy," I told her. "How am I going to manage?"

Katy did her best to reassure me, but when she saw that she was making no progress she consulted with the floor's senior nurse, who sent out calls for a resident psychologist and a chaplain.

Shortly both visited me, though not together. I'm sure they gave me their best advice, but I have no recollection of what it was.

It was eventually Mrs. O'Leary who came to my rescue. She must have been on her ten o'clock break when I heard that soft Irish voice at my bedside.

"So it's been your toughest day, I'm guessin'," she said, "and that's because tomorrow you're goin' home." She sat on the bed and grasped both my hands.

"Did they tell you?" I asked.

"No, I don't need to be told," she said. "I've seen a lot of patients who've suddenly lost their sight—auto accidents, young 'uns playin' around with guns—you name it. I've seen the bravest come apart at the seams on the day they're told they're goin'

home. What frightens them—what's scarin' you, darlin'—is how
to make it on the outside. Am I right?"

"Oh yes, yes," I whispered as I leaned forward into Mrs.
O'Leary's ample bosom and soaked the lapels of her cleaning-
lady uniform with tears. She stroked my hair, patted my back,
rocked me, and cooed soothingly into my ear.

"There, there, me darlin', you're goin' to be just fine, and the
good Lord will still be wantin' to use your love and all your
learnin'."

With my crying under some control I told her, "You're wonderful, Mrs. O'Leary. You could be giving lessons to the psychol-
ogists and some of the chaplains, too."

She snorted, "Get along with you, darlin'. I was but fourteen
when I leave school. Had to help me mother run the farm in
County Kerry—that were after me dad died. I was milkin' five
cows and churnin' cream afore I were ten years old. Not much
time for book learnin'. But I'd like to tell these chaplains somethin'; I'd tell them to make their rounds and come a-visitin' at
three in the mornin', not at three in the afternoon. That be the
hour they're most needed."

She chuckled so deeply that the bed shook. "Tell the truth,
sometimes I feel more like a chaplain than a cleanin' woman.
Course I'm raised Catholic, yer know. I doubt if the Holy Father
in Rome would give much thought to makin' me a chaplain."
Another wonderful laugh, and so infectious that I joined her.

She heaved herself off the bed, and from the way it sagged
when she had sat down I guessed she weighed in at over two
hundred pounds. I painted her face on the canvas of my mind.
She surely had three chins, Irish rosy cheeks, and blue-button
eyes that almost disappeared when she laughed.

"Best be goin'," she said.

I was so reluctant to let her go that I felt for her hand, but I realized that she was at the door.

From there she turned and said, "I'll be lookin' in on you later, darlin', to see how you're farin'." A new thought struck her. She asked, "How's that story of yours goin'?"

On one of her earlier visits to my room I had told her of how, for essentially therapeutic reasons, I had spent wakeful hours trying to recapture the events of my life. She had been so intrigued that she had said she would pass the idea on to other patients.

Now I told her that I had not made much headway lately. Weighed down by the challenges of going home, I was not inclined to get back to the story.

"Ah, no, darlin'," she said, "you need somethin' to be thinkin' about this night—somethin' good. Now tell me what be the happiest day of your life? A Christmas, maybe? Your weddin' day, likely?" She chuckled. "Ah, you're already smilin' as you think about a happy day. What is it you're thinkin', darlin'?"

My answer was firm. "I'm thinking about the day my daughter Joy was born," I told her.

"There you are!" said Mrs. O'Leary triumphantly. "Tonight you be givin' yourself a treat. Keep your mind on sweetness. You be thinkin' about that little lass of yours, and she'll be leadin' you to dreamland."

After she had closed the door, I heard the sound of Mrs. O'Leary collecting her cleaning equipment and then the flapping of her slippered footsteps retreating down the hall.

I took Mrs. O'Leary's advice. I thought about my daughter.

Joe and I were two years into our marriage when Joy was born. Although I remained healthy, I could not free myself of a deep concern, at times closer to a phobia, that my baby would be born with some physical defect.

I should have shared this foolish concern with my physician.

Had I done so I would have learned that it is a pregnancy problem not uncommon among women who work with the physically and mentally disabled.

There was no moment in my life of greater relief and exaltation than when the doctor who delivered my daughter told me that she was normal in every respect—"not just ten toes and brown eyes, but absolutely perfect!"

Mrs. O'Leary's soporific worked marvelously. On my last night in the hospital I enjoyed the most restful sleep I had had since being admitted as an inpatient.

I was dressed and ready well before Joe arrived at ten o'clock the next morning. When he phoned from the lobby to say he was signing the insurance documents and discharge papers, I felt so good that I told the senior nurse I wanted to make my own way to the entrance to meet my husband.

"Certainly not," said the senior nurse (unfortunately, it was Katy's day off duty). "You'll find you're much weaker than you imagine. Besides, it's a hospital rule that patients must be wheeled out in chairs." There was an unintended sting when she added, "Your husband's got to get used to waiting on you."

When Joe reached my room, a couple of other nurses came to say good-bye. An orderly had my suitcase. Everyone, including Joe, was awkwardly hearty.

"Sure you've got everything?" Joe asked as he swung the chair to the door.

"Can't help you there," I replied.

I was conscious of Joe glancing about him before he said, "There's a card or something on the nightstand. Do you want it?"

The nurses were obviously eager to be about their business and I was anxious to be on my way. "I've no idea what it is," I told him. "Probably just a tissue."

Joe picked up what he described as a folded piece of lined

paper carrying a penciled note. He asked me if I wanted him to read it and I told him to go ahead.

He read: "Good-bye, darling lass. Glad to see you sleeping like a babe. To have a vision you don't need no eyes. Your heart will tell you what to do. I'll be praying for you. The Lord has good sweetness and blessings for you. I be sure of this."

An embarrassed silence followed. I put out my hand to Joe for Mrs. O'Leary's note, and I pushed it into the pocket of my jacket. It has been a sadness for me that somehow the note written on cheap paper was lost. It may have been left in the jacket pocket when it was sent to the cleaners.

But Mrs. O'Leary's prophecy—for that's what it seemed like to me—was so etched into my mind that I was to recall it again and again, word for word, as my future unfolded—into a time of anguish beyond my reckoning, and a time of sublime contentment beyond my imagining.

7

But Why Not Me?

❧

As we drove home on that crisp, mid-March morning in 1984, I could sense immediately that something was seriously troubling Joe, and that whatever it was, it was creating strain between us. I knew that it couldn't be his proximity to a blind person, for he had lived and worked for seven years with people with vision loss. Joe's chatter about inconsequential things and the pitch of his voice convinced me he was evading some issue that he really needed to talk about.

My first guess was wrong. I asked, "Are you as concerned as I am, Joe, that I'm going to be a burden to you?"

Had I struck him his reaction could hardly have been sharper. He shouted, "For Pete's sake, Joan, how can someone I love be a burden?"

I leaned across the seat and put my cheek against his arm.

"Thank you, honey, that's wonderful to hear," I told him.

"I mean it," he said quietly.

"Oh, I know you do," I said, and then I pressed the question: "But there is something on your mind, Joe." I allowed a ten-second pause before I added, "Isn't there?" The addendum triggered a response.

"Yup. Okay. I've been asking myself why the heck you?"

"Me what?"

"You know what I mean," he said, his voice rising. "Why the heck should you be . . . be . . . "

"Blind! Say the word, Joe. I've gotten used to saying it about myself."

He slowed the car. I thought he was going to pull it to the side of the highway, but apparently there was traffic ahead. I could smell diesel fumes.

His lighter mood was now gone. Almost harshly he replied, "I can say the word 'blind' and all the euphemisms—sightless, vision loss, you name it. No, what I want to know is why *you*?" He sucked in his breath, a recognized signal that anger was surging. I knew he needed to express his deepest feelings—angrily, if that would help.

He continued loudly, "There are more than two hundred and fifty million people wandering about this country and most of them have never given a damn about helping blind kids, about helping anybody. Why should you be singled out to lose your sight? That's what I don't understand. It's pretty hard to talk about a loving God when this happens. The woman who wrote that note to you—the one you asked me to read—did she have any answers? Oh, sure, she's going to pray for you—I've no quarrel with that. You know, I was raised Catholic, but I never heard any priest or nun explain why the best people, often the most caring people, get slapped down the hardest. You asked me what's worrying me. It's not just worrying me. It's been tearing at my guts. Why you, Joan? Why you? For God's sake, why you?" His last phrase was bellowed.

He was breathing heavily. I wasn't sure what to say—not immediately. My mind was jumbled, confused, scared. Silently, I asked God to help me give Joe some sort of acceptable or helpful answer. One thought came to mind like a quick benediction.

Softly I said, "Joe, the only answer I have is, 'Why not me?'"

When he didn't respond I continued, "If I were to imagine that I'm so good that nothing bad should happen to me, wouldn't I be putting myself above everyone else? What I definitely don't believe is that God is punishing me. If I believed that, then I'd be questioning my faith. We're not living in heaven. We're living in an imperfect world."

When I paused, Joe interjected, "Go on. I need to hear this." His voice had quieted.

I said, "I think the answer is just that simple, honey. Why not me?"

A long silence was broken when I said, "I suppose almost everyone who is, as you put it, slapped down hard, is strongly tempted to ask, 'Why me?' I'm thinking of Mr. and Mrs. Holman who lost their only child to leukemia last year. You remember them. A lovely couple who live in that house near the post office—the one with a prize rose garden. They'd waited twenty years for that child. Then it was taken. I think the little boy was only nine."

Joe made no comment, so I continued. "I guess that little girl who was raped and murdered out there on the Waterloo road never had a chance to ask, 'Why me?'"

"But the girl's parents did," interjected Joe.

"Yes, I guess they did," I agreed. "'Why us?' But their question didn't bring the little girl back. And you know what Mrs. Holman did when her little boy died? She's now got half a dozen little boys. She's one of our most loyal volunteers at the Braille School. She spends hours with that autistic kid, Terry."

We were silent for a while; I was praying silently that my answer to the "Why me?" question had satisfied Joe. Oh please God, help Joe—help both of us—not to be bitter, never to be bitter.

These thoughts were so earnest in my mind that I was hardly conscious of speaking aloud when I said, "I'm hoping that in some way my loss of sight can be used for the good of others."

I was aware of Joe turning his face toward me. Was he thinking about my answer? I yearned to see his expression. I said, "Obviously there'll be things I'll have to do differently, like getting Joy to school. But I believe the Braille School kids might feel they've got a staff member who better understands their challenges and difficulties."

Joe asked, "You really want to go back to the school?" He was genuinely surprised.

"Absolutely," I said emphatically. "I shall beg and plead and smile."

Joe reached out with his right hand and touched my knee. "The smile alone should do it," he said. I was glad that his anger had waned, perhaps some of his worry, too.

In a non sequitur he now told me that some of the trees were already in bud. For both of us, springtime was our favorite season. I had a spasm of heart pain as I reflected that for the first time I wouldn't see the April greening of the town—nor the tulips and daffodils in the park, nor . . .

I jerked my mind away from these negative thoughts. In one

of my more enlightened moments at the hospital I had solemnly promised myself that I would never, but never, allow myself to be sucked into self-pity, not only for my own sake but for Joe's and Joy's—and indeed for everyone I encountered. I had seen how indulging in self-pity was a tortuous route to losing love and friendship. A few streets distant from our home a once popular and vital woman had destroyed her marriage and her relationships with her family and friends when she became so embittered by a mastectomy that she had alienated herself from the kind of healing care and contact she most needed.

I opened the car window and allowed the clean air of the prairie to play on my face and stream through my hair. I surprised Joe when I told him I knew exactly where we were.

A short laugh now. "Have you been kidding us all along?" he asked.

"I'm learning to make use of my other senses," I told him. "A couple of minutes back we hit that big pothole that should have been filled in a year ago. I've just picked up the smell of coffee from what has to be Hank's Diner. That means that hideous wrecked-car dump must be out on the left. Correct?"

"Almost," said Joe admiringly. "We've just passed the wreck dump."

"Well, that's one thing I'm glad I won't have to see again," I told him.

"Do you want a running commentary on the view through the windshield?" he asked. "We had a light snowfall yesterday. There are still patches of white on north-facing roofs."

My throat tightened. "No," I told him, "I'm not quite ready for a travel talk. It just makes me feel—well—too nostalgic or something."

We didn't speak again as we drove through the pretty town. I tried to picture the red bricks, the neat shops, the 250-year-old oak trees with their gnarled trunks and still bare limbs, a glint of light from the river, now probably in spate. A couple of minutes later Joe swung the car left and the sound of gravel under the tires told me I was home at last.

Then Joy was in my arms. As we entered the house I picked up the perfume of spring flowers, perhaps hothouse grown, and the smell of Irish stew, doubtless the gift of a colleague or friend.

Joy pushed a vase of daffodils under my nose. I breathed in the scent. "Beautiful," I told her. An obviously nervous baby-sitter read a florist card's message from Joe's folks. Then Joy was lifting up a pot of sweet-smelling hyacinths and the baby-sitter helped her describe the pastel colors.

"There are some more flowers in the dining room and upstairs," said Joy, who was jumping up and down as if she were riding a pogo stick. Joe now read the names and messages from other cards. Louise, my dearest California friend, had wired flowers to me, as had both my brothers and their wives.

It was all too much too soon. Like the almost overpowering perfume of the flowers, I felt overwhelmed by love—indeed, I would have fallen had I not grasped the banister.

"I need to rest for a while," I said. "They warned me at the hospital that my legs would feel wobbly for a time. It's great to be home."

I pulled myself up the stairs and, quite drained, flopped on the big bed. Joe left for his duties at the school. Joy snuggled next to me for a few restless minutes. It was good to hold my daughter in my arms again, but I was relieved when she left to play with a friend.

In the now quiet house I recalled that summer six years earlier when I had arrived in Vinton as Joe's bride. Joe had been working at the Braille School for a couple of years and already seemed to have made friends with half the community. He was a valued member of a basketball team and a softball team, both made up of school workers and local business and professional men.

I recalled, too, the first day of my being employed at the Braille School. I was appointed housemother of a dorm of ten legally blind boys whose ages ranged from six to eleven. Two older, experienced (though unqualified) aides who were to work under me were understandably nettled over having to take orders from a naive, though college educated, twenty-six-year-old who had had little experience of caring for sighted children and no understanding at all of how to help blind children become civilized citizens.

Fortunately I'd had enough sense to recognize that I would fail miserably at my job unless I could win the confidence and perhaps the friendship of the two motherly aides who would have to be my principal teachers.

Actually, while lying in my bedroom and remembering my first days at the Braille School and my bridal days and nights with Joe, I fell asleep. But in telling my story this seems to be as good a place as any to speak of my professional work.

8

Born of the Heart

§

The job of looking after ten small boys for eight hours a day—especially when they were unable to run away—had sounded simple enough. I was to find out differently.

I had not been aware, either, that many children born blind are multi-impaired, for blindness is often caused by prenatal problems or birth traumas. In the dorm to which I had been assigned house-mother, five of the young boys were not only legally blind but were handicapped in other ways, too. One was autistic, another mildly retarded, a third was obliged to wear leg braces, a fourth had to use a wheelchair, and another had the use of only one hand.

While all the boys were legally blind (meaning that the mildest case had vision of only twenty over two hundred), about half had (as I now did) some light perception from peripheral or minimal central vision.

I had immediately turned to the two motherly aides, confessed my ignorance, and pleaded for their help in teaching me
how to care for the boys. The training I needed is not found in
textbooks. The effective caring for and bringing up of blind children is a skill born of the heart and consolidated only by hands-
on experience.

Indeed, my very first lesson was as simple as teaching a sightless child how to make his bed. One of my aides demonstrated
hand-over-hand instruction on tucking in a sheet, smoothing a
blanket, and correctly placing a pillow.

By watching his mother, a sighted child can learn to make a
bed in two or three sessions. A blind child might take six months
before making a bed that doesn't look like the bottom of a laundry chute.

The same patience, I learned, was needed in showing a blind
child how to tie a shoelace, how to keep himself clean, the effective use of toilet paper, the sorting of clothes, and so on.

One of the toughest lessons for a blind child is learning to eat
without resembling a zoo primate. The kids were invariably hungry, and taste is one of the heightened sensual pleasures when sight
is lost. Of course the boys could not see each other, and they had
little interest in impressing sighted table attendants. Yet training in
eating in a mannerly fashion—using, for example, a hunk of bread
as a "pusher" to the fork—is among the most important learning
experiences for a blind child if he is to be socially acceptable.

The instruction and care at the Braille School occupied
twenty-four hours a day. The dorm teaching of self-sufficiency
was no less important than the classroom teaching. Although I
was in charge of the dorm, I didn't sleep there myself. My hours
of work usually coincided with Joe's. Both of us went into action
when academic classes were over for the day.

Although my early official responsibilities were limited to domestic care and social skills, it had seemed very important to me to learn all I could about the classroom teaching and other activities of the children. Joe taught me much, of course.

The highest peak of excitement for most of the children was to go camping under Joe's leadership. I would tag along, too, and found the experience fascinating—like watching kids, boys and girls, put up their own tents. Many sighted campers could have learned a lesson in the importance of, for example, a tight guy rope. Joe taught them to fish the streams and lakes, to manage a boat, to identify woodland sounds, and so on. He was very firm with any child who did not measure up to what he believed was his full capability. I was pained to see one child in tears after Joe had scolded him. When I had protested his severity, Joe had pointed out that he may have saved the child from death or injury because the boy had crossed a street without listening for traffic. He always gave a big hug to a child he had reprimanded.

At one of my early activities at the school Joe gave me a lesson I needed and one that I would not forget. His recreation department was holding the annual St. Valentine's dance at which the Sweetheart King and Queen were to be crowned. The students themselves voted for what was the equivalent of homecoming king and queen. Since football was obviously not a Braille School sport, Valentine's Day was set aside for the election of the students' royalty.

I had, by now, gotten to know a good many of the 120 students on campus, but there were still a few I had not befriended. Among these was Joyce, a girl with rounded shoulders, buck teeth, bulging and very obviously sightless eyes, and mouse-colored hair so thin that her scalp was visible.

The election count and crowning ceremony were being held

at the gymnasium, and Joe was emceeing the occasion. Excitement mounted as Joe came to the mike to declare that the vote had finally been tallied. The name of the king was no surprise. He was a tall and handsome youth who had done well both in wrestling and academics. Then Joe announced the name of the queen. I couldn't believe what I heard.

Her! I thought, as the gym rocked with cheers. Joyce, who was just about the plainest girl on campus, had been chosen by her peers to reign over the festivities!

When, later, I had mentioned to Joe my surprise at the choice of the queen, he had tartly retorted, "Honey, you haven't learned yet that beauty is in the eye of the beholder, and on this campus the kids look more than skin deep."

The classroom teachers were more amazed than amused when I started to turn up in their classrooms. I did so, not to learn about United States presidents, nor the names of the Canadian provinces, nor yet the rudiments of math, but because I felt it important to understand what the kids were being taught and how they were being taught. I needed this knowledge if I was going to be able to help them with homework or other projects. One veteran teacher told me that I was the first dorm parent to sit in on a classroom lesson.

I also felt it was important to learn braille, which I did in my spare time. It is not all that easy to translate the dots that make up the braille alphabet into letters, phrases, and pages, but in due course I became a certified braillist.

My understanding of braille came in handy when I began classroom teaching. Then I took some blind students to the public schools downtown. This was known as "mainstreaming," and it was the aim to give as many as possible of the Braille School children an opportunity to study at, even graduate from, public schools.

Being able to read and write braille allowed me to transcribe the homework instructions of a public school teacher into notes that could be understood by the blind students, and then to transcribe the work written by the blind students in braille back into phrases that could be understood by the public school teachers.

I loved my work, initially as a dorm parent, later in a classroom setting, and then as a professional liaison staff person between the dorms and the classrooms, a job which also kept me in close touch with the parents and families of the children.

I joyfully discovered my own wellspring of compassion, and I found myself especially drawn to the kids most in need of time and tender loving care. I had not before experienced a richer reward than that of seeing a child's development and progress following hours, days, or weeks of patient and sometimes painful instruction.

The blind children unwittingly gave me lessons which were to prove priceless in my own unforeseeable years ahead—lessons in patience, perseverance, and humor.

One of my dorm boys was a mischievous but lovable ten-year-old named Blake. It was Blake who owned a whoopee cushion that emitted rude noises when sat upon. (He caught me three times with this one.) It was Blake who brought a couple of caged white mice back from a vacation, and then let them loose in the dorm. It was Blake who was always being reprimanded for using "dirty words." I don't think he knew the meanings of most of them, but he loved to shock the staff.

One day I was assigned to take Blake to the University of Iowa Hospital's ophthalmology department (the very same!) to be fitted with new prosthetic eyes. As a child grows, so do his eye sockets, hence the need to replace prosthetics from time to time.

Appointments were running well behind schedule. As Blake and I waited in a room filled with perhaps forty people, many of them elderly, the boy became restless. He asked me how everyone else was killing time. I mentioned that they were reading magazines. Blake discovered a magazine rack next to his seat. A few moments later I was aware of a heavy silence in the waiting room. Glancing over the top of my journal I saw that all eyes were fixed on Blake. He had removed one of his glass eyes and he was now holding it delicately between thumb and forefinger as he pressed it against a magazine page.

"Blake!" I exclaimed. "Put it back now!"

Before popping the glass eye back into its socket, Blake gave the room his best urchin's grin and said, "Too bad! I can see so much better that way!" He seemed genuinely disappointed that nobody laughed. But Blake and I giggled all the way home.

Another boy who besieged and conquered the inner chambers of my heart was Terry, who had been rejected by his wealthy parents—obviously because he restricted their lifestyle. Terry had a bewitching lisp. To him I was always "Mith" Beringer and his struggle to pronounce Mississippi left a geography class in an uproar.

Perhaps the toughest of my duties in the course of my five sighted years at the Braille School was to receive the new children. Mostly they came to us at the age of five or six, some older, a few younger. Most stayed at the school until their late teens.

It was beyond my ability to imagine what went on in the mind of a child when he became aware that he was being abandoned by his parents—the couple who had, since his birth, protected and guided him through the darkness of his existence.

I did see the agony on the faces of most parents when they

handed over their child to the school's keeping. I could almost hear the parents asking themselves how they could conceive of giving guardianship of their beloved child to a young, blonde girl who, to them, looked as if she should be playing tennis, skiing, or lying on a beach! Indeed, there was one occasion when a father ran back and would have snatched his son from me had he not been restrained by his wife.

Unfortunately, there were rare exceptions to parental love. I happened to be within earshot when I heard one couple already whooping it up as they returned to their new Jaguar. From the distance I could hear the screams of the little girl they had dumped at one of the other dorms. These parents were obviously thrilled at being able to return to their social life, no longer fettered by having to care for their handicapped child.

The Braille School was designed to be a home away from home. The main building was constructed in the last mid-century, and the mellowed walls seemed to carry a patina of caring and healing. When I was appointed to the liaison position, one of my duties was to take parents and other visitors on a tour of the buildings and to give a presentation on how the children would be helped and cared for. I did so proudly because the school was not only handsomely furnished and equipped with state-of-the-art facilities, but it was also staffed by exceptional people.

By the fall of 1983 life was great. In my liaison position I was doing the work I most enjoyed, work that kept me in close touch with the children, their parents, the dorm staff, and the teaching staff. I was often invited to give presentations on the work of the school to service clubs, church groups, women's associations, and the like.

I put together a program that I felt helped people to comprehend what it was like to be blind or seriously visually impaired. For these lectures I took along a suitcase full of equipment, including braille books, slate and stylus (the process students used for taking notes), beeper balls and beeper Frisbees, talking calculators and gogglelike glasses that distorted a lens to give tunnel vision to the partially sighted.

As for the Joy of my heart, as I always thought of our blonde, effervescent daughter, she was well out of babyhood and becoming her own engaging personality.

We were really a quartet, because Jay, my stepson, spent so many weekends with us and was fully embraced into the family.

Each day, when I counted my blessings, I ran out of fingers, and each Sunday, when I gave thanks for them at church, I almost ran out of amens. Of course, I had known from first memory that God was in His heaven, and I now had every reason to believe that all was right with my world.

Christmas of 1983 came in with the merry sound of carols and sleigh bells. Joe and I welcomed in a new year of high promise—hailed 1984 with a kiss and champagne and in the company of wonderful friends.

Then came that bitter morning in January, the day before my thirty-second birthday, the day when I was dressing my daughter for her preschool, the morning when Joy's pink socks looked white, so strangely white!

9

Sparrows and Grandmother's Bowl

§

A few days before Joy's pink socks had seemingly been drained of their color—that first sign that my life's trail was dipping rapidly from sunlight into twilight—I had made a promise to the Braille School's peewee wrestling team that I would be at their annual match against their number one rival, a school about ten miles from Vinton.

Nothing and no one could have stopped me from keeping this promise. As I reflected sardonically to Joe across the breakfast table, this was to be my "first firm blind date." In fact, I'd been home from the hospital only three days when the date for the big match came up. By phone I made arrangements with the bus driver to swing around to our home after he had collected the peewee team and their supporters at a dorm.

As soon as I heard the crunching of gravel under the bus tires I went outside the front door. The bus driver jumped out to give me a guiding elbow, but before he did so I was aware of a little figure alongside him. Then a small, sticky hand gripped my own and a very familiar lisping voice said, "It'th me, Terry, Mith Beringer. I juth wanted to tell you how very thorry I am about your eyes. I gueth all we can do, Mith Beringer, ith to hope."

I felt so absolutely overwhelmed by the little boy's sympathy that I choked up. Terry, now eight, and who, as I remembered so well, looked like an angel, had lost his sight in an appalling accident when he was an infant. But here he was, grasping my hand, giving me his compassion.

"Oh, Terry, Terry," I cried, "how wonderful you are." I knelt down in a patch of melting snow and hugged him. "You won't understand what I mean, Terry, but in your heart you've got the answer to so much of the pain, the misery and the grief in the whole wide world."

The other kids who had remained in the bus gave me such a warm welcome, too. Their calls came to me like tossed rose petals. "Welcome back, Mrs. B.! I hope the doctors were nice to you. We missed you very much. We love you, Mrs. B."

The natural humorist, Blake, wasn't joking when he said, "You're kind of like one of us now, Mrs. B."

In all my time at the Braille School I'd not experienced such a feeling of camaraderie. Yes, I told myself, we are in it together, bonded by our special challenges, our frustrations, our longing to make it in the sighted world.

Wrestling is one of the very few sports that the blind can participate in and enjoy. There have been some outstanding amateur blind wrestlers. Here I would like to report that my peewee team won their match against their old rivals but they didn't, and this time they lost—in spite of my cheering myself hoarse from the bleachers of a gymnasium.

On our journey back to Vinton, we talked about winning and losing, and how losing could be a spur in the flank. Indeed, our dialogue on the bus home could have been a locker room morale booster at a superbowl.

In those first days and weeks at home there were moments when I felt lost, beaten and depressed, but Terry's lisped encouragement—"All we can do ith to hope"—rang out in my head like an encouraging cry from the bleachers. I would falter and fail many times, but I promised myself that I would always pick myself up and go back into the fight. Then I would experience a surge of strength and confidence. I would, I told myself, never, never give up.

Understandably, Joy was initially very confused by my inability to help find things she had mislaid—her crayons, for example, or a picture book. But there were other activities, such as bathing her, that I could manage with the same facility as I had had before losing my sight.

Especially for our small daughter's sake, both Joe and I made every effort to keep laughter in our home. Joe could, for example, pull pennies out of his ears and then make his ears wiggle. One evening when I was bathing Joy, Joe came home from work.

"Hi, girls!" he said cheerily as he pushed open the bathroom door.

"Hi, honey!" "Hi, Daddy!" we responded.

As Joe approached he pretended to trip on a throw rug. A moment later he was sitting fully clothed in the bath facing Joy

who was, of course, squealing with laughter. Years later, when
Joy recalls this Chaplinesque scene, her laughter is still close to
hysterical.

Memory shortens the months and, sometimes, the years, but
another recollection of Joe's creative ways of bringing fun and
excitement to our home now comes to mind.

This incident was in midwinter and Jay was spending the
weekend with us. Joe announced that the whole family was
going to go camping. Outside, the snow was lying piled high.

"Camping!" we exclaimed in unison.

"No problem," said Joe. "We'll camp in the family room." •

And so we did, Jay and Joy setting up their own small tents,
which were furnished with sleeping bags. A pizza supper was
ordered by phone and the only light permitted was from the
blazing log fire. Joe and I slept on a pull-out couch. It was not
difficult to imagine that we were out in the prairies and that we
could hear the howling of wolves.

When Mom and Dad came to visit I think they were properly impressed on finding the housekeeping running so smoothly.
I showed them how I arranged Joy's clothes and my own in closets so that I could find them readily. I demonstrated the arrange-
ment of food in the refrigerator and in the kitchen cupboards. I
could find and reach for a carton of milk or a box of rice as easily
as I could have done had I been sighted—unless, as too often
happened, Joe or someone else had put the staples back in the
wrong places.

Joe feigned amusement on taking over grocery shopping. He
expressed glee when he found bargains.

Friends and neighbors rallied round, too. A knock on the
front door and the smell of hamburgers or roast chicken heralded
the arrival of yet another nourishing meal.

I was learning, too, how to use my white cane effectively. I had taught so many children mobility and how to tap their way to a classroom or up a flight of stairs that I had a head start as I began to use a cane myself.

It was a victorious day for me when I first walked downtown unaccompanied. No place was far distant in little Vinton, but Joe was concerned when I announced that I was going to walk to the pharmacy to purchase what was euphemistically called "feminine hygiene." I guessed Joe would be embarrassed by having to make such a purchase.

When I set out I insisted that I didn't want any help at all. I suspected that Joe followed me at least some of the way. If he did so, he didn't let on.

I had, of course, walked the route from home to the shopping area very often in the past—one block east, one block north, then four blocks east.

Now mobility skills would be fully tested. In a manner I had previously prescribed for others, I swung my cane from fence to gutter. Ah, yes, I told myself, here's the fire hydrant near the second corner, and this is where the roots of that big tree are breaking through the concrete pavement—a place requiring special care—and that barking has to come from the Restons' German shepherd. Here's the corner where I turn left. Okay! Now four blocks east. Remember to count them.

Fortunately, the sight of a blind person tapping his or her way down a Vinton street was not rare. As I approached the shopping area I was conscious of people stepping out of my way. When crossing a street I listened carefully for traffic, then took advantage of the offer of the arm of a female stranger. Otherwise I made the short walk unaided.

Was this the door to the pharmacy or the shoe-repair shop? I pushed it open. The friendly and familiar voice of the pharmacist greeted me. My sigh was not so much one of relief as one hailing a personal victory. I did it by myself! Wow! Marathon winners or cross-Channel swimmers could not have experienced a warmer glow of glory!

Another early thrill was to be told by the school's top administrators that they wanted me to keep my professional job as liaison staff person. I would continue to link the dorm staff to the teaching staff. But since there were some duties that I would now be incapable of undertaking I was given a few different responsibilities. Among these was to spend a couple or more evenings a week in charge of the study period at the library.

It was in the library that students, particularly those taking classes at the public schools, could find a quiet place for homework and, at the same time, make use of a wide selection of reference books—typically talking encyclopedias.

When practical, and when asked, I would try to give students help with homework, but increasingly I would encounter students who came to the library simply to talk to a staff person who, as one of them put it, "really understands what being blind is all about."

One evening when on my library stint, I was approached by Betty, an exceptionally intelligent sixteen-year-old who, since her arrival at the school, had been first in her class. But as she approached the corner table where I usually sat, she was obviously distressed.

Eventually Betty blurted out, "An absolutely awful thing happened to me today in the lab."

"Tell me about it," I said softly.

A shuddering sob came from Betty before she uttered the word "birds."

"Birds!"

Three tissues later she whispered, "It was so humiliating; I'd always thought that birds were about the size of my thumb. But in the biology lab they've got a stuffed seagull and a stuffed crow. I couldn't believe what I was feeling. They were the size of . . . of my head!"

I still couldn't fathom the reason for Betty's tears, and I said so.

"But don't you see, Mrs. Beringer, I thought I was pretty smart, and today I realized how ignorant I am. I thought that because birds go 'cheep-cheep-cheep' they had to be tiny. I've been getting straight A's in math, English, history, and geography, and yet I didn't know that . . . Well, I felt I should be thrown back into kindergarten."

It was a new lesson for me on how little understanding those born blind have of dimensions. Unless it has been explained to them or unless they have been able to measure things themselves, those born blind have little conception of shapes and sizes.

It was very different for me, because memory came instantly to my aid when someone mentioned a church steeple, say, or an oil tanker or a tree or an ostrich or whatever.

That evening and in many evenings that followed, Betty and I had fascinating discussions on the sizes of things. Since she was tak-ing a course in biology she was particularly interested in animals. To explain the reach of a giraffe I took her to a wall in the library and asked her to stretch her hands above her head. I explained how, when a giraffe was munching leaves from a tree, it could reach up to four or five more times than the distance between Betty's fingers and her toes. She was quite stunned by this revelation.

We had a speculative and philosophical discussion as to whether it was better or worse to be born blind, as Betty was, or to lose one's sight when one was older.

"I don't know what I miss," submitted Betty.

"And I miss so much of what I used to see," I told her, giving an example of how, the previous morning, Joy had spoken about the clouds "looking like lambs playing in a blue field."

I said, "I ached to see not only what my daughter was looking at, but to see her animated face as she gazed upward at the scudding clouds."

"Ah," said Betty, claiming some advantage. "I never have those yearnings. How can you miss what you've never had?"

"Oh no," I responded, "I'm the lucky one. Someone speaks of—what?—an owl flying over a field, and I've got an instant picture in my mind—a moving picture, at that. I see not only the flap of the owl's wings but the blue-green fir trees it's heading for."

I didn't want to press my argument because I felt sure that Betty—and everyone who is born blind—is far less fortunate than those who lose their sight when they are past early childhood. For instance, in the days when I was sighted, one of the toughest teaching lessons was to persuade children who had been born blind to make appropriate facial expressions—expressions they had never seen. I think especially of Robbie, who took long months to learn to smile. When he came to us he had a grimace that scared young sighted children. Our task was to help give Robbie's smile warmth and humor.

In any event, Betty proved to be a quick learner. Although she wasn't able to call on memories of things once seen, she eventually graduated cum laude from a university, and today she is an outstanding teacher of blind children.

In these fast-paced times it is tough enough for sighted people to keep up with a changing world, and I'm not thinking only of atlases that have to be radically redrawn every few years. But I do miss seeing new architecture, the shapes of new automobiles, and, particularly, new fashions.

Even though on a modest budget, I had always tried to keep my wardrobe up-to-date. If the arbiters of fashion had decreed that hemlines should be above the knee, mine were lifted (as often as not, before I went blind, with the help of scissors and sewing machine). If the spring or fall dresses were shown to have the hemline at the calf, my hemlines dropped, too.

Current copies, borrowed or bought, of *Elle* and *Vogue* used to be on our coffee table, but now that I was no longer able to look at sleek models showing off the latest styles from London, Rome, Paris, or New York, I was forced to rely on the taste of clothes-conscious friends, who also helped me decide on the waving, cutting, highlighting, or shaping of my hair.

Having the right clothes for the right occasion has been close to a fetish for me, and while, as I've already explained, I was careful to place clothes in a known order in closets and drawers, I did make mistakes. It still remains a concern that I might appear in public wearing a pink shirt with a yellow skirt (or vice versa), or that I could show up wearing an outfit better suited to a Halloween party than to a ladies' luncheon.

Socks are the bane of my existence. I tried to be particularly careful when placing socks in a drawer. Blue socks were parked in the left-hand top corner, white were in the middle back area; black were in the bottom right corner, and green, red, and yellow were assigned to special places too.

However, as Robbie Burns, the Scots poet (among my favorites) reminded us, "The best laid schemes o' mice an' men gang aft a-gley." Blind women are much more likely than either mice or sighted men to have their schemes go a-gley. They certainly did so one afternoon when I was scheduled to give a talk on the history of the Braille and Sight Saving School to a group of out-of-state visitors.

The black knee-length socks I needed to go with my outfit were not where they should have been, and since I was already running late, my frustration shifted into desperation. I yelled for six-year-old Joy to come and help me. She was a little slow arriving, and by the time she reached my bedroom door I was hurling socks wildly all over the room. From the doorway there came a sobering cry.

"Mommy, Mommy, stop it!" screamed Joy.

Mortified, I hugged my daughter and begged her forgiveness. "I'll try so hard never to go crazy like that again," I promised her.

Joy was eventually able to find a matching set of black socks, one sock at the far end of the bed, she told me, and the other on the windowsill.

Only a little late for the visiting VIPs, I was tempted to tell them about the Crazy Clarabell I'd been ten minutes earlier. However, I acknowledged that there was no humor at all in behavior that had scared the daylights out of a little girl.

But often laughter over my mistakes was genuine and shared, especially when I made what Joe described as my "banana peel boo-boos." Understandably, we ate out much more frequently these days. While I enjoyed cooking a meal, the challenge to do well was considerable, and all too often I over- or undercooked because I was obliged to rely on timing, texture, and odor. I gave up counting the number of times my best efforts at the stove went down the garbage disposal.

One evening, after we had eaten at a family restaurant, Joy took me to the ladies' room. When we came out again, she was a few paces ahead of me. Assuming the blurred figure at the desk was Joe, I grabbed an arm and made for the door. The arm did not belong to Joe!

We never did learn whether the man whom a blonde was

propelling to the door of the establishment and out to his car had assumed I was a lady of the evening, because Joe caught up with us, pulled me away, and possessively marched me to our own car. Had the stranger's wife or a friend watched this comedy, we wondered how he had managed to explain away a simple case of mistaken identity.

I've experienced several similar identity problems. One that still gives me a chuckle occurred on a beach. When I left the surf after a swim, my "pigeon compass," as I called it, was off by several degrees. I lay down on what I thought was my towel, but the man alongside me had a much hairier chest than Joe's, and his exclamation seemed to be in Dutch or German. I was just very glad I didn't understand it!

I could laugh at these blunders, but there were many days when frustration or impatience walked at my shoulder—and at Joe's big shoulders, too. I can't recall why both of us were so edgy on the evening my parents paid us a visit, having made a detour in their journey to visit us, but it was obviously one of those days.

Dad, who, by his nature and through long pastoral experience, was supersensitive to human frailties and to the problems of relationships, took advantage of a hiatus in the living-room conversation to give us the kind of advice both Joe and I needed.

He turned his face to me and asked, "Joan, do you remember the story of Job?"

"Job—oh, er—yes," I stammered, "I think so. All those horrible things that happened to him. Everyone knows about the patience of Job."

"Yes," agreed Dad, "but not many people know or remember what happened to him."

Joe interjected, "As I remember, Job had some great days when he was an old man."

Dad chuckled. "Right on target. The King James words

are 'The Lord blessed the latter end of Job more than his beginning . . . and Job died, being old and full of days.'"

I asked Dad, "What made you suddenly think of Job?"

Another chuckle. "Truthfully, I was really thinking of you
two. You see, patience has never been one of the easier virtues.
We're all tempted to want the right things to happen yesterday."

"Guess so," said Joe.

Dad allowed a pause for pondering before he said, "But I
wasn't thinking so much of patience as I was of what happened
to change Job's fortunes."

"And you're about to tell us," I said, laughing.

"Yes," said Dad, who by this time had already shifted Joe and
me out of the sulky mood in which he and Mom had found us.
"Yes, I sure am. This is a free Thursday-night sermon. No col-
lection plate."

Now we were all laughing.

Dad continued, "There is one key verse in the story of Job—
a verse that is usually overlooked. It's the tenth verse of the last
chapter. Job's fortunes changed when he stopped thinking about
himself and started thinking of others. Few people have had
more to complain about than Job did. But the day came when he
stopped scratching his boils and prayed for his friends who were
in trouble. And that's when everything turned around for him,
and when, in your words, Joe, Job moved into great days."

There, in our living room, I appreciated as almost never
before the caring quality of my father, and his wisdom, too.
Importantly, Joe moved closer to my father that night. The time
was drawing near when the new and richer relationship between
the two men was to prove so valuable.

The next morning, after Joe had left for his office, Joy and I
walked my parents out to their car, each of us as determined as
ever to put on brave faces at our parting.

For some reason, just before Dad pulled the car out of the driveway, I became disoriented. I smiled and waved, but when doing so I was looking the wrong way.

To me, when Joy referred to it afterward, my mistake was of no consequence and quickly forgotten. But years later Mom told me that when she and Dad had caught sight of me looking east instead of west they had pulled to the curb farther down the street. Then they had cried their hearts out.

It seemed to me that whenever I was down, whenever I was in danger of being drawn into self-pity, I was guided—perhaps by my guardian angel—down softer pathways. I'm so grateful for these interventions and benedictions, given when most needed and when least expected.

In seeking an example, I'm thinking of that early summer morning when I so yearned to see the leafy trees, the flowers— especially the lilacs—the sky, the sight of children at play, that I burst into tears. Joe, who had not yet left for his office, was naturally perturbed, especially when I was unable to explain the reason for my sadness. He was satisfied, however, when I hinted it was just "a woman's thing" and that I'd soon be fine. He left me alone. But I wasn't fine.

Then I felt myself almost drawn to a balcony, not often used, on our second floor. There, suddenly, I became aware of being serenaded by a heavenly chorus.

What first caught my ear was the chattering of sparrows from what had to be the broad-leafed maple tree near the road—the one from which Joe had slung a swing for Joy. Then my ears became attuned to other instruments of the avian orchestra. Soon I was entranced by trying to isolate one bird call from another. I wondered what was giving them such zest? Were they still court- ing, or were eggs newly hatching, or were they just expressing good feelings about this beautiful day?

I was conceited enough to believe (as did, of course, Snow White when she was out in the woods!) that the birds were singing for my particular pleasure. At the correct moment for an aria, a mourning dove began its soft cooing, its song as melancholy as a Sibelius motif. Then a woodpecker, which was patently not keeping its eye on the conductor's baton, rat-a-tat-tatted away at the bark of, I believed, the alder tree on the far side of the woodpile.

I counted them on my fingers—seven different birdcalls! Cocking my head this way and that, and even applauding a flute-crisp trill or whistle, I obviously gave the impression to Mr. Foster, the octogenarian pensioner who lived right across the street, that I was signaling trouble.

Mr. Foster, who knew about my blindness, shouted up to me, asking if I needed help.

"Oh, no!" I shouted back (momentarily silencing half the orchestra). "I'm just fine. I'm just enjoying the birds singing."

I'm not sure whether the old fellow heard me, because his eardrums were very leathery and he rarely used his hearing aid. But in discovering how acutely I could now focus my own sense of hearing, I was on a sort of high—and not one, as I later reassured Joe, that was caused by over-medicating.

Naturally, Joe was confused by my mood swing. He had come back early from his office to check on my well-being. He had, after all, left me in tears. He returned to find me singing. But how to explain to a man with a tin ear that I had been marvelously entertained by a feathered Sibelius, a full chorus of sparrows, and a musically undisciplined woodpecker!

"And I didn't tell you about the love song of an amorous robin?" I exclaimed to my husband.

"No, you didn't, and I don't want to hear it," he said as he switched the TV to a sports program.

I did catch his interest, though, when I told him I was cooking him a special dinner, and not one from the freezer. Neighbors and colleagues had kept our freezer well stocked with cooked meals. But on this evening I had breasts of chicken in the oven. There'd be roast potatoes and green beans, too.

Preparing the meal was not that difficult for me, for I had helped many blind children—boys and girls—to become familiar with the kitchen and to be competent cooks.

The square baking dish was where I had last left it, in the cupboard under the silverware. The olive oil was in the cupboard above the stove. I tore a sheet from the paper towel roll, put the spout of the oil bottle on the towel, upended the bottle, then spread the baking dish with oil. I did the seasoning by pouring salt, pepper, and minced onion on the back of my hand to gauge the approximate amount. I poured butter melted in the microwave over the chicken.

Setting the oven temperature was really no problem. I knew the angle of the dial when the oven was set at 350 or 400 degrees—the most common setting of an oven when baking. On this first occasion I did cheat. I called in a neighbor to check my setting, which, she told me, I had angled correctly for 350 degrees. I set the timer for one hour. Where special care was demanded was in removing the roasted chicken from the oven. For blind people it is essential to use elbow-length mitts to protect the arms from burns. The previous evening a school coworker had brought me a brand new pair of these.

The meal itself, which included a salad and ice cream, was a triumph. We even had candles on the table. I'd insisted on these. All of us replete, Joe and I then put Joy to bed before we returned to clear the table and do the dishes.

It was at the sink that the accident happened. I was drying

my grandmother's cut-glass bowl (which had held the green salad) when it slipped through my fingers and splintered on the tiled floor.

"Oh, how could I have done that?" I cried out in disgust and horror. I was kneeling on the floor, feeling for slivers, when Joe responded.

"Yes, you should have felt that the bowl was soapy. You'll have to do a lot better than that."

The excitement of the day, the fun of the evening, suddenly evaporated.

I lay awake that night until the small hours. I wondered how a now-imperfect wife was going to be able to meet both Joe's expectations and her own.

10

"I'm Going to Die"

§

While I was embarrassingly deluged by people using synonyms for *courage* and *stoicism* (if only these well-meaning folks had known how frail I often felt!), few gave a thought to how tough Joe's life had now become.

Here was a man so strong, vigorous, and masculine that he gave the impression of attacking life with a rapier; here was a man who possessed the compassion needed to be a good teacher of the severely handicapped; and here was a man whose time and activities were now restricted by unanticipated duties and concerns.

He rarely complained about having to do the grocery shopping, or driving me anywhere I needed to go, or so many other chores, but in one depressed moment, when he seemed to be speaking more to himself than to me, he revealed what most weighed on his mind.

He said, "I work all day with the blind, and I come back at night to a blind wife."

As I've mentioned, Joe was a perfectionist, a trait that can be admirable in some vocations and circumstances (was not Michelangelo so described?), but one that often exacerbates difficulties. Yet his high standards encouraged me to strive to improve my capabilities.

The three of us (or the four of us when Jay was with us) had many exhilarating times together, including memorable camping and beach vacations. Together, and with pride, we watched our daughter move through those especially enchanting middle years of the first decade. Often, when I would inquire as to what was so engaging his attention that he was silent for a long period, Joe would respond that he was watching Joy at play.

I recall his once saying, "Our daughter is so pretty, so graceful, so happy, that I could spend the whole day simply watching her."

This observation was made when we were on a beach and Joy was building a sand castle or something. On such occasions I most coveted my husband's eyes. I would enjoin him to tell me more—"Tell me what she's doing this very moment. Oh, tell me, tell me . . . "

When Joy was six, I gave up my professional position at the Braille School. One reason was that I felt it important to be available to Joy at all times. Her school was close, and there were few moments of my day I more enjoyed than school recess, when Joy would likely bring half a dozen of her friends to see me—or, perhaps, to sample my home-baked cookies.

If the weather was good, I would sit on the upstairs balcony and wait impatiently for the welcome invasion of the six year-olds. Then I would hear the cries of "Hi, Mom!" "Hi, Mrs. B.!" "Hi, Mrs. Beringer!"

How my heart would warm to those treble salutations.

There were other reasons for giving up my job. One was that Joe had just been promoted. But the most compelling excuse was that my energy level was near its lowest ebb. Arthritic pain had surged, and I was constantly aware again of pleurisy.

Because of my physical problems I was obliged to spend more time visiting medical specialists who were trying to balance my medications—notably steroids.

As I sadly handed in my resignation to the Braille School superintendent, Dennis Thurman, I gained his kindly laughter when I said, "You won't believe this, but I've come to the conclusion that I'm not Superwoman!"

Both Mr. Thurman and my immediate supervisor, Mary Beth Young, gave me what they described as "total freedom of the campus" and assured me that I could visit any dorm, any classroom, the library, or any other facility at any time. They both also said good things about my work at the Braille School.

Joe supported my decision to give up my job, and because I had become so much more efficient in running our home—and I loved being a full-time housewife and mother—he was now freer to enjoy outlets for his seemingly inexhaustible energy.

Joe had always been a sports fanatic and, in his off-duty hours, if he wasn't playing basketball or softball, there were TV sports programs on one channel or another—some of them, I began to believe, created or transmitted especially for him.

In the spring of 1988 I noticed that Joe was losing some of the edge to his enthusiasm, not only for his work and sports but for social engagements too. He would find a thin excuse for not playing basketball with his highly competitive friends, or for not going to a Friday-night barbecue.

One afternoon, when his favorite baseball team, the Los

Angeles Dodgers, were featured at spring training, I was amazed to find Joe asleep on the living-room couch. The game was on the screen and the volume was, as usual, too loud. But Joe was snoring!

There were other omens. He was uncharacteristically irritable. He snapped at Joy, and Jay, too, when his son was visiting. The incidents came more frequently and often without reasonable cause. I had long gotten used to his rebuking me for clumsiness or for one failing or another, but his rebukes now carried a hurtful sting.

I excused him because I knew his sinuses were acting up. Joe had suffered from allergies all his life, and I believed that the reason they were so much worse this year was because more spores or molds had been liberated by the springtime warming of the soil.

What triggered my anxiety into real concern was a suppertime incident. We had a full table because Mom and Dad were visiting again and so was stepson Jay. Between us, Mom and I had prepared one of Joe's favorite dishes—pork chops. I was certainly expecting a compliment when Joe said sharply, "Where's the applesauce?"

It was his tone of voice that shocked the table into silence.

I attempted to smother the awkward moment by speaking up lightly. "How silly of me," I acknowledged. "I forgot that the jar was empty, but there's another in the basement."

Eager to make amends, I hurried to the basement. The next thing I knew I was flat on my back. The playroom door had been left half-open. My forehead and right knee hit the edge of the door at the same moment. I was badly shaken and very sore.

Before returning upstairs with the applesauce, and taking a moment to rub the bruises, my anger gathered. Back at the table,

I told the company what had happened and then angrily told Joy and Jay to try to remember to close all doors. (A half-open door, I should clarify, is one of the more common domestic perils for the sightless.)

I was shocked and shaken when Joe said, "It's your fault anyway. Didn't you spend years teaching blind kids to go slowly? Why don't you practice what you preached?"

The rest of the meal was eaten in silence. My parents and the children were obviously no less upset than I was. But I hurt for Joe, too, because I knew he was ashamed of his retort.

Later, when my parents and I had a moment alone, I explained about the sinuses. "He's really not himself at the moment, and he's been having awful headaches."

When Mom asked why Joe didn't go and see a doctor, I told her, "Because he doesn't like doctors. He doesn't trust them. He feels that the doctors could have done something to save my eyesight if they'd been quicker with treatment."

I added quickly, "That's what Joe thinks. It's not what I think."

When Joe and I were in bed that night, I raised once again the problem of his sinuses and headaches. I said, "Honey, they seem to be so much worse this year. I hear you using that nasal-spray thing all the time. You know very well that you shouldn't be doing that. There used to be and probably still is a red-lettered warning about squeezing the thing no more than four times a day."

Joe grunted. "Nothing seems to help anyway. It's the headaches that get to me." It was strange to find myself in the role of consoling this strong and usually self-contained man. After a long pause I asked him if he would do me a favor. Would he please see a doctor?

"Just Dr. Anthony," I said. "Remember, he's your friend."

"No quack has ever done anything for me," he protested, but I could tell from his voice that his opposition was weakening. I pressed my advantage and gained his promise that if within one week his headaches were no better he would see Tony Anthony.

Exactly one week later I heard him on the phone speaking to the school office. I heard him say that he wouldn't be going to work that day as he had "a cold or something."

I moved to his side. "What's really the matter?" I asked.

"Another damn headache," he admitted.

"Then you have another call to make."

"Huh?"

"To Tony Anthony—you promised."

"Oh yeah, maybe later."

I lifted the phone off the cradle. "Right now," I insisted as I gave him the doctor's number—one of about fifty important phone numbers I now had registered in my head.

Later that afternoon Dr. Anthony gave Joe a prescription drug to help dry out his sinuses, but he also made an appointment for Joe to see an ear, nose, and throat specialist in Cedar Rapids, about half an hour's drive from Vinton.

Three days later, a Cedar Rapids ENT man gave a quick diagnosis. The cartilage in Joe's right nostril had grown and it had shut down the air passage. The minor problem would require simple surgery.

Surgery was scheduled for June 10. For me, this was not early enough, as I became increasingly distressed by Joe's mood swings. I didn't express my anxiety aloud. In fact, I gave Joe every encouragement to enjoy himself in his pain-free spells.

It was his idea—and one I heartily endorsed—to take the family to a Twins' ball game in Minneapolis. What balm to my ears to hear Joe explaining the niceties of the game to Joy and her half brother. I suspected that Joe had earlier swallowed a mouthful of painkillers.

On the drive home, Jay asked his father why he was going so slowly. When Joe didn't reply, I asked him if he had a headache.

Joe turned to me and said blisteringly, "Okay, Joan, you drive!"

I gulped and replied softly, "That doesn't sound like you."

He touched my face—his gesture of apology—then said quietly, "It's not a headache. It's just—well—for some reason I'm seeing double." He pulled in a deep breath and added, "Don't worry, I'll get us home. Damned sinuses. Surgery will fix 'em."

The day before the surgery, Joe's parents, who were always supportive, joined us in Vinton. It was they who drove us (Joe and me) to St. Luke's Hospital in Cedar Rapids.

The septoplasty procedure lasted only half an hour. The surgeon told us that everything had gone well. Joe's nose would be sore for a few days, and he would stay in the hospital overnight just in case there was some postoperative hemorrhaging. When Joe had recovered from the anesthetic I hugged him and assured him that he was back on track.

The hospital allowed me to sleep on a cot in his room. They granted me this favor because I was known to several members of the medical staff. It was at St. Luke's that I had undergone a number of tests to try to identify the lupuslike condition that had destroyed my eyesight. Ken and JoAnne went home to be with Joy.

The cot which they had placed alongside Joe's bed was comfortable enough, but I didn't sleep well. I kept thinking that I, not Joe, should be in the bed, and that I, not Joe, should be getting the attention of the nursing staff. Something seemed absurdly wrong.

The next morning the surgeon looked in and told Joe to keep off the basketball court for a while. He also asked Joe to report back to his office in a couple of weeks.

It was a long two weeks. The nose did not heal, as promised, and Joe's headaches intensified. The double vision remained. On the tenth day after what was supposed to have been a simple procedure, Joe had a bad hemorrhage. He went to the bathroom to clean up.

When he eventually came downstairs he said, "Funny thing, but I could swear that my right eye looks much bigger than my left eye."

"Probably bruising caused by surgery," I suggested.

"Probably," he replied, "but you'd think—oh, forget it."

But I couldn't forget it.

When the two-week checkup day arrived, Joe insisted on driving us to the surgeon's office, adjacent to St. Luke's Hospital.

"What about the double vision?" I asked anxiously.

"Oh, I'm fine when I keep my right eye closed," he assured me. He feigned a light mood and said, "We only need one good eye between the two of us."

Joe was a surprisingly short time with the surgeon. I naturally thought all had gone well and that his nose was healing normally.

"What happened?" I asked as he pulled me from my chair.

"Got to take this to pathology," he said flatly.

"What's this?" I asked.

"A small vial. Contains some tissue from my nose."

Tissue! Pathology! The words sounded alarmingly ominous.

The pathology department was in the hospital's basement and it necessitated a long walk. A doctor in an elevator and two nurses in a corridor recognized me. They asked how I was far-ing. I forced smiles. Purposely I didn't introduce the man at my side. Joe was very calm (or in denial) as he handed over the vial to a pathology department nurse.

I had come to hate the distinctive smell of hospitals. For me it was the cloying odor of pain, tragedy, and grief—so much so that when I now bought soap or household detergents I first made sure that they didn't smell like the antiseptic cleansers used to scrub hospital corridors or the hands of the medical staff.

Because the doctor had said there would be no pathology report until mid-morning on Monday we returned home, but our weekend was shadowed by thoughts that someone had looked through a microscope at a tiny piece of Joe's flesh.

Joe returned to the Cedar Rapids hospital on time on the Monday morning. I sat by the telephone.

It was about eleven-thirty when Joe phoned. His voice was firm but his words froze me.

He said, "I'm on my way to the University Hospital at Iowa City where I have a one o'clock appointment." A pause for an intake of breath. Then, "I have a malignancy."

"Oh, Joe!" It was all I could manage to exclaim.

"Look, I'm running late," he said. "I'm calling from a truck stop." His voice was still level. I could hear the roar of a big rig's engine nearby.

I swallowed the huge lump in my throat and asked, "Should I call your parents?"

"Do that," he said. "Just my folks—oh, and your folks, too. No one else." A pause and another big intake of breath. Then, "I love you."

I heard his phone click. A moment later Joy came running to ask me if she could go down the street to play with a neighbor's child. She spotted my tears.

"Mom, what's the matter?" she asked. "Was that Daddy on the phone?"

I wiped my cheeks on my sleeve. "Yes," I said. "He told me that—that he loved me."

"Oh!" said Joy. "Well, it's okay then. I can go and play with Peggy."

"Of course," I said, "and if they ask you, you can stay for lunch."

I was compelled to wait about twenty minutes before I was sufficiently in control of my emotions to call Joe's parents. I managed to avoid breaking down as I told them only what Joe had told me. They were ready to drive to Vinton immediately. However, I suggested they wait until Joe called me and we knew more.

Then Joy reappeared. With the directness of a seven-year-old she said, "Mom, I want to be with you when you are sad. You are sad, aren't you, Mom?"

"Yes," I said.

She was eager to comfort me. When we sat down side by side on the couch she borrowed one of my own phrases used when comforting her. She asked, "Will it help you to tell me about it?"

I tried to smile as I said, "Darling, you're only seven years old!"

She giggled. "You're feeling better, aren't you?"

I squeezed her. "How could anyone *not* feel better when they're with you?"

I thought of how, since the age of three, Joy had had to shoulder unusual responsibilities. She was three years old when she first lead me to ladies' rooms at restaurants and airports. At six she was reading me menus and important notices, even struggling to read me letters.

She was also a beautician's apprentice—at least, that's what I called her as, each morning, she checked my makeup, making sure, for instance, that there were no globs of mascara on my lashes!

And now my seven-year-old was asking me to share the reasons for my grief. However, I found myself quite unable to do so. I was glad that Joe had asked me not to tell Joy about the diagnosis.

Although I'd been expecting the phone call, when it eventually came in mid-afternoon the ring was as alarming and as alerting as a gunshot at midnight.

"It's me," Joe said.

"Yes! Yes?"

"I have cancer." His voice was as flat as a robot's.

My heart was pounding.

"Cancer of the sinuses," he said.

A five-second pause; ten seconds; fifteen seconds. What was happening? Was he still there? Yes, I could hear his breathing. Then, "They want to take out my right eye."

"Oh, no! No! No!"

Another long and dread-filled moment. Then, "I'm coming home."

So taut was I, so absolutely horrified, that any comforting response I might have been able to give him remained locked in my throat.

His voice was still dead when he said, "Did you hear me? I'm on my way home."

"Yes, Joe," I rasped. "I heard you."

"You haven't told Joy?"

"No."

"Good. I want to tell her."

"Yes. Do you want your parents here?"

"Yep."

"Drive carefully—very carefully."

"Yep. See you soon."

"I love you, Joe."

"I know."

When the phone had rung Joy had been riding her Big Wheel in the yard. I was aware that she was now beside me and gripping my leg. I was still holding the phone.

My words were spoken aloud when I prayed, "Dear God, please help us. Please help us all."

My mind was very slow in receiving the full shock of Joe's words. Joy knew that something was terribly wrong.

Scared, she asked, "Has Daddy had an accident?"

"No," I told her, "but he's sick, very sick."

"Is he in the hospital?"

"No. He's coming home. He'll tell you about it." I was surprised that my voice sounded almost normal. I told Joy to go out and play on her Big Wheel for a while as I needed to make some phone calls. When I heard the front door close I called Joe's father, who said that he and JoAnne were on their way.

Then I called my parents. Because Dad had recently retired, he and Mom had moved back to Bakersfield, California. There they now owned their first home. It was Dad who answered. This time my voice did break, but I managed to tell him the tragic news. Dad asked if I thought Joe would like him to call back that evening. I told Dad that Joe would be sure to value his call very much.

On our hearing the car arrive, Joy and I rushed out to greet Joe. After a brief exchange of kisses, Joe distanced himself from us. I guessed that while he was driving home he had thought out the best way of handling his arrival. He was clearly determined to keep his emotions on a very tight rein.

Once inside the house he sat on his recliner and, in simple terms, he explained what had happened at the University of Iowa Hospital. He could as well have been speaking about a school project. He would certainly have been more animated had he been speaking about baseball. He mentioned the name of the specialist who had examined him, a Dr. Douglas Dawson.

"I liked him," he said. "He used a model of a head to explain where this tumor thing is growing. He's my kind of man."

I'd never before heard Joe pay tribute to any physician.

He turned to Joy. "A tumor is like an enemy—a very nasty enemy. The doctors are going to attack it so that it won't be able to hurt me anymore."

Joy asked if the doctors would use guns to kill the enemy.

"Yes, sort of guns," he said, "and some very sharp knives."

"Like swords?" asked Joy.

"Sort of like small swords," he replied gently.

The conversation continued at this simple level until Joy was satisfied that the doctors were going to help win the war against a bad enemy who was hurting her beloved Daddy.

It was an extraordinary conversation, and for me, a new revelation of Joe's courage. Here he had been talking about the greatest crisis in his life, in our lives, in the same tone and manner as he told bedtime stories to his daughter. Since he had not mentioned to Joy that he was going to lose an eye, it was little wonder that she was satisfied and went upstairs to bed.

Of course the dialogue was on a different level when Joe's parents arrived late that evening. While I was busy making them sandwiches, Joe explained in technical detail how the doctors would try to save his life. The atmosphere was heavy with shock, sadness, and disbelief.

Only when we reached the bedroom did he loosen the tight

reins he had kept on his emotions. Both of us were wordless as we held each other closely for half an hour or more, I trying desperately to hold back my tears and to control the trembling of my limbs.

Then Joe whispered, "When your father spoke to me on the phone tonight he recited the Twenty-third Psalm." He paused so long that I wondered whether that was all he was going to say. I made no response because I did not trust my voice.

But then Joe continued. Still in a whisper, he quoted a couple of the fabulous verses: "He leadeth me beside the still waters . . . Yea, though I walk through the valley of the shadow of death I will fear no evil. For thou art with me . . . "

After another long silence Joe said quietly, "I need to believe those words to be true. You must help me to believe them, sweetheart, because . . . because I'm going to die."

11

The Longest Day and a Silent Night

§

Joe battled for his life for seven months. In my returning now to the scenes of his battleground, I find myself thinking of a black-and-white movie I saw on TV when I was very young. I cannot recall the name of the movie, or the names of the stars who acted in it, or even the story, but I do remember a knight in full armor leading his army against a foe. Although the knight was mortally wounded, he went on fighting and encouraging his soldiers until he could no longer lift his sword. Only then was he struck down.

Yes, that was Joe. His courage blazed.

From that first grim diagnosis, he knew the chances of his surviving were very small. His principal surgeon, Dr. Douglas

Dawson, must have observed Joe's strength, for he did not mince his words.

Joe was given three options. The first was, in effect, to do nothing, to eschew surgery and medication, except for drugs to subdue the pain. If this were his choice, the doctor told him, he might live for two, possibly three, months. The second option was to go for surgery alone. He would, as he already knew, lose an eye. The chances of the cancer returning within the year would be high. His third option was to undergo the surgery and follow up with chemotherapy and radiation. There would be a chance that he could go on living.

No promises were given that Joe would even survive the radical surgery by a team of ten or more specialized doctors and technicians. We were told that the surgery would last twelve hours, possibly even longer. The cancer had already moved its destructive tentacles into the frontal lobe of Joe's brain. A section of the brain would have to be removed.

Joe had selected his option immediately. I was beside him when he said, "Of course I choose the third option. For the sake of my family I want you to do all you can to prolong my life."

Ironically, the man who gave Joe the only positive news was Dr. Corbett, the physician Joe had so disliked when he was in charge of me. Joe now saw Dr. Corbett as a trusted member of the surgical team being mustered for the dangerous and complex operation.

Dr. Corbett told Joe, "While there is no way of salvaging the right eye, the left eye is absolutely clear of cancer."

Joe was certainly smiling—I could tell—when he turned to me and said, "Honey, we can manage on one working eye, can't we?"

Early in the evening before the surgery Joe settled into his room at the University of Iowa Hospital. The adult members of his family held a brief prayer service at his bedside. Dad had flown in from California. Dave, our minister from Vinton, had joined us, too, as had Joe's parents and his brothers. We had left Joy with friends. We all held hands as Dave prayed. For me, four words, "Thy will be done," remained poised in the air over Joe's bed.

Then the large family group left Joe and me alone. We held hands for a spell, then Joe said, "Sometimes I forget to tell you that I love you."

"I know," I said, "and I should say those three words more often too."

Joe then reminded me, although I'd not forgotten, that the following day would be our tenth wedding anniversary. He said, "Next year, honey, we'll be in a better place than this—I promise you."

I was calm until Joe said, "I wish I was as strong as you, sweetheart."

"Oh, but you are," I said urgently. "You're stronger." I clasped him then and found that he was trembling. That Joe was deeply afraid made the moment especially moving for me.

That night in bed I sat up and bowed my head as I thought that without fear there can really be no courage. Joe's vulnerability and trembling made him all the braver to me.

The next dawn began my longest day—a day of what proved to be sixteen hours of surgery. Sometimes by phone from the operating theater to the waiting room, sometimes in person, Dr. Dawson gave us progress reports. He and his colleagues were, he said, amazed by how fit Joe was. His heart, blood pressure, and other vital signs had given them no concern at all.

At one point, and at my request, the doctor had traced with his fingernail on my own skull just what area of Joe they were

Joe and I at our wedding, July 1978.

A Beringer family photo before the storm. Jay, five and a half,
Joy one and a half.

Joy and I at her fourth birthday in 1984 after my vision loss. Life goes on regardless of challenges.

A reunion with my brothers, Bob and Jon, in 1984 just after my vision loss.

Joy and I in Bakersfield on the three-wheel bike giving our dog,
Lady, a ride.

Joy and I at my wed-
ding to Jim in 1992.
(*Kevin Fahey*)

With Jim and Joy, June 1992. A beautiful day to begin a happy new life. (*Kevin Fahey*)

A Stuebbe family photo at Jim's and my wedding in 1992. Flanking me (*left to right*), my brother Jon, Mom and Dad, and Bob. (*Kevin Fahey*)

Mom and Dad at the wedding. (*Kevin Fahey*)

Jim and I on our wedding day. (*Kevin Fahey*)

High school football star Jay Beringer, fall 1993.

Joy caught me preparing our 1993 Thanksgiving dinner in our kitchen in Tucson— just an ordinary mom.

Jim, Joy, and I in our backyard in Tucson, fall 1992, a "pet" giant swallowtail butterfly on Joy's cheek.

Joy and I with a four-legged friend, Christmas 1993. We both love to ride.

cutting. I was appalled when the doctor's nail moved in an arc across my head from one ear to another, and then around the socket of my right eye, then down my nose and cheek to my upper lip. The doctor explained further that Joe would lose half his upper palate and some teeth. I expressed my horror that Joe would look terrible, not to me, of course, but to the world. The doctor assured us that plastic surgery, a dental plate, and, in time, a prosthetic eye would re-create an almost normal face, and that, when the swelling had decreased, the casual observer might not give him a second glance.

We were cautioned that because a section of the brain had been excised, Joe might be in a coma for some days. But on the following morning when Dad and I were first permitted to visit Joe in the intensive care unit, he recognized us and even thanked us for coming.

Joe was in the hospital for two weeks. His doctors were surprised by the pace at which he regained strength. However, his last day at the hospital was a particularly traumatic one for him. His family, who had been with us frequently, was asked by a nurse to leave the room. She was, she said, going to show Joe how to clean out his eye socket—a task, she cautioned, that had to be performed with a special solution and a Water Pik twice a day.

Now, for the first time, Joe was to see his face without an eye patch or bandages. He asked me to stay with him, and added wryly, "At least you, honey, won't keel over."

The nurse removed the eye patch and led him (so I was being told by Joe) to a wall mirror. Then I heard Joe hiss with horror as he looked into his wound. A moment later and he was beside me on the bed and breathing hard. He gasped, "If I'd seen a face like that on a man lying in the street I would have said he was dead."

All I could do was squeeze his hand.

The nurse, who had surely been specially selected for duties as difficult as this one, pulled Joe to his feet again. She said gently, but with authority, "Mr. Beringer, if this wound gets infected you're in big trouble. If you want to recover, if you don't want to be quickly back in the hospital with a septic head wound, you must learn to cleanse your eye yourself and very thoroughly. Let's try again."

Instruction on the use of the Water Pik took quite a while. I tried not to think of what was going through Joe's mind as he irrigated his eye socket. When he was finally ready to leave the hospital he was wearing an eye patch and also a cap to cover his shaved head.

One of his sportsman brothers greeted him by shouting, "Kick butt, Joe."

Joe laughed. It was the first laugh I had heard from him in more than a month. He said, "I already have K-B'ed."

But that night, when we shared a bed again, Joe was far from laughter when he said, "Honey, I want you to know that I'm going to leave you soon. I'm just glad I've been given time to put things right, to put my insurance papers and my will in order, that sort of stuff."

I felt that Joe understood my silence.

After a long time he said, "I've been thinking about that time when your Dad came here and he talked about the Book of Job. Remember?"

I nodded.

"The most important thing that happened to Job was that he stopped scratching his boils, and he began to think about other people. Do you think those boils were on Job's butt? I once sat in some poison ivy, so I know what a very sore butt can be like. I had to eat my meals standing up. Now where was I?"

"You were quoting Dad," I said, my voice half muffled by the pillow. I didn't want Joe to hear me in the event that I sobbed.

"Ah, that's right. Yup, with what's happened to me and what they've done to me, I could spend my time being a jerk. I don't plan to be a jerk, and I think what your Dad was saying was that if you want to stop being a jerk, start thinking about other people. Right?"

"Right," I said.

"We've especially got to be thinking about Joy and Jay. We've got to be strong for them. You, too, sweetheart."

"Yes," I said. I was crying now, but so softly that he didn't seem to hear me.

The very powerful sleeping pill he had swallowed half an hour earlier began to take effect. He began to slur his words. Over and over again he said, "Good to be home . . . good to be home."

When I knew he was asleep I got up, grabbed some blankets, went downstairs, and made up a bed on the couch in the living room. What I had been concerned about was that in my turning over in our queen-size bed I would awaken Joe. When he slept he was pain-free. When he was awake he was rarely, if ever, free of pain.

Before dawn I was awakened by a bellow from upstairs. My peripheral vision could not pick up a glimpse of light from the window. I gathered my wits and became scared. Had something horrible happened to Joe?

As I stumbled into the bedroom my mind was relieved when Joe demanded, "Aren't you still my wife?"

"Of course."

"Then why didn't you sleep with me?"

"Because I—"

"Because nothing. I want you beside me. I need you beside me. Okay?"

"Okay."

"Then climb back in."

Later in the morning, while Joe was cleansing his eye socket and after Joy had gone off to school, I went alone to the second-story balcony. Since that long-ago spring morning when the birds had given me a concert, it had become a sort of sanctuary for me. It was a good place to think and to experience what I described to myself as a spiritual in-filling.

Invariably I took up a Juliet-on-the-balcony pose. I leaned my elbows on the wooden rail and cupped my chin in my hands.

The tang in the air was a reminder that fall had begun; so, too, were the sounds of dead leaves scratching the sidewalk as they were whipped into eddies by wind gusts. A large leaf from, I guessed, the maple tree brushed my neck. People with sight would not, I thought, have noticed this soft caress. They would have been absorbed by the colors of the fall—the yellows, golds, and reds of every hue—the colors I could no longer enjoy.

Every day now I was waiting for the honking of the geese migrating down from the north. If I were lucky, Joy or Joe would be with me when the geese arrived overhead. We'd exclaim together. We always did.

While enjoying, then, the scents, the touch, the sounds of the fall, I allowed my mind to free-float, as it were. This was the way of things when I sought and relished these quiet interludes on the balcony. I first gave thanks for blessings, for the care and support of family and friends, and then I spoke the names of people in need—Joe's name first, of course, then Joy's and Jay's. I asked for help for Mr. Peterson, across the road, who had had a mild heart attack. There were a dozen others whose names I offered to the Throne Room.

Then in my "free-float" moments I experienced an in-filling of peace, a reassurance that God had not let go of my hand, and never would. The quietly flowing stream of my thoughts encircled Joe once more. For the first time I knew in my heart—though my mind and my lips would continue to deny it—that Joe was in the autumn of his days, that Joe would, as he himself had told me, leave me soon.

This understanding that Joe was dying did not preoccupy my thinking. There wasn't time for morbidity, nor the need for it. Each day I was challenged to be a good homemaker and mother. Also, Joe's courage helped ward off hovering specters of gloom.

Only two weeks after he had returned home, only four weeks after he had undergone sixteen hours of surgery, I found Joe dressed, with collar and tie, and rattling the car keys.

"What's happening?" I asked.

"I'm going to work," he replied chirpily.

"You mean you're going to the Braille School?"

"What a quick mind you've got," he said, laughing and bending to kiss my cheek. "You surely recall that I'm an assistant administrator, and I suspect that after my long absence the in basket is reaching the ceiling."

"But Joe, you can't—"

"I can, and I'm going to. My eye patch is in place. My mustache has grown back, and although my hair looks a bit tufty, I intend to keep my cap on. The kids don't give a hoot what I look like, and to the staff I'll look—well—rather rakish."

"But Joe, you're not yet—"

His hand was over my mouth, effectively smothering protest and concern.

In those early weeks back from the hospital Joe's main frustration was his difficulty in speaking or, more accurately, in being understood. Part of the surgery, as I've mentioned, had been the removal of half his palate, but the plate which had been fixed over the roof of his mouth to allow him to eat, as well as to speak, would become loose.

On the phone, especially, he had to talk slowly, enunciating each word. If he removed the palate plate, which he was obliged to do when his mouth became sore, only Joy could understand him.

He now spent much more time with Joy than he used to, and with Jay when his twelve-year-old son was visiting. I'd often find him sitting on Joy's bed late at night while our eight-year-old was fast asleep.

He explained, "I can't see enough of her. I want a thousand photographs of her in my mind. Soon, those photos will be all I'll have." Of Jay he said, "I want to share ideas with him—thoughts that may help him when he's grown up."

He made it clear that he had sorted out his priorities. He was eager to start radiation. He would, he told me, do anything the doctors proposed if it would usefully extend his life—"by a month, a week, a couple of days." He added, "But I sure don't want to be kept alive if I'm just a vegetable."

One evening when he came home from an administrative meeting he was patently deeply upset. After he had slumped into his recliner I asked him what was wrong.

"Can you believe it?" he shouted. "We wasted an hour talking about staff parking problems! Here we are, two hundred staff people claiming to be trying to help blind kids cope with the sighted world, and we spend half our meeting arguing over who is going to park where. I nearly threw up. Wish I had."

Joe changed. He was different in so many ways. He was making every day count and, I suspected, counting every day that was left to him. He was more caring, more courteous, and even, it seemed, and when occasion offered the opportunity, more humorous.

For a period an ear infection related to the surgery caused him to lose his equilibrium. After he was given some medical attention at a hospital, we had to walk quite a distance to the car. To prevent himself from staggering, he was obliged to lean heavily on me. I could hear other people moving about, and I mentioned to Joe that we must look like that well-known picture of wounded Southern soldiers returning home from the Civil War.

"No," he said, "we look more like a couple of drunks." So saying, he burst into a song and purposely slurred his words. I wished I could have seen the faces close by. As he drove us home, his laughter was deep.

He claimed to be pleased when he started to lose weight. A neighbor lady offered to alter his suits and pants. He was delighted when friends told him that he looked in better shape than he had for years—possibly true because he had previously been badly overweight.

For a while only I knew how exhausted he really was and how sick he became following the radiation treatment. Then suddenly, after Thanksgiving (when we had made the six-hour journey to his parents' home in South Dakota), Joe became very frail. It was as if an overnight storm had swept away the leaves from a stalwart oak.

Joe, in his mid-thirties, was now entering the winter of his days. He gave up going to the Braille School. Often he failed to clean out his eye or could not be bothered to do so anymore. I was haunted by the warning that he could get a septic socket.

Also, I had to struggle every day to persuade him to eat. All he wanted to do was sleep.

Our home now became strangely quiet. We rarely turned on the TV. Joy and I tiptoed around the house. And Joy no longer brought in friends from school. How often in daytime did I climb the stairs to find out if Joe was still breathing? How many times at night did I awaken and anxiously listen for the sound of his breath?

But the heroic knight was not beaten yet. In the middle of December a Braille School houseparent and friend, Elaine, phoned to say that "Joe's blind kids" had asked if they could come and sing carols to their beloved Mr. B. These were the kids he had taught to wrestle. These were the kids he had taken camping.

Except for when he crawled to the bathroom, Joe had not gotten out of his bed for ten days.

To Elaine on the phone, I held back my answer for so long that she asked, "Are you still there, Joan?"

"Yes," I said, "but I'll have to ask Joe."

"But they're coming this afternoon," said Elaine. "They'll just sing outside his window. Perhaps he could give them a greeting. They'll be at your house in about three-quarters of an hour."

I promised to give Joe the message.

Joe was in such a deep sleep that I was reluctant to awaken him to his world of pain. He was never now without a headache, too often a savage one.

It took three shakings of his shoulders to rouse him.

"The kids are coming here?" he asked, half dazed.

"In less than an hour," I told him, "but you don't have to worry. Joy and I will welcome them. We'll get some candy. It's okay. Just go back to sleep."

When Joe made no reply I assumed he had gone back to a drugged sleep. A neighbor took Joy to buy candy canes. I was in the kitchen when I heard an unusual thumping noise. Joe was coming downstairs! He was on his hands and knees. He had dressed himself in a sweat suit.

"Oh, Joe," I cried out, "you didn't have to."

He reached the bottom of the stairs at the moment Joy burst through the front door and cried out that the carol singers were now only two blocks down our street.

Joe instructed Joy to put on all the houselights. I mentioned that the kids wouldn't see the lights.

"But I will," he replied, "and Joy will, and the neighbors will."

As soon as the kids arrived and began to sing "O! Come All Ye Faithful" Joe opened the door and leaned against the door frame. A horseshoe-shaped circle of kids stood out there in the bitter cold. Joy walked around the circle, handing out the candy canes from a basket, and I, with tears streaming down my cheeks, walked behind her and gave each child a hug.

Between carols the kids called out, "Hi, Mr. B.!" "Merry Christmas, Mr. B.!" "Get well, Mr. B., 'cause we miss you."

The kids cheered when Joe called back something that sounded vaguely like "Merry Christmas." I guessed that his palate plate had slipped again.

Finally, the blind children broke into "Silent Night." I'd never heard the words sung more sweetly. I surely never will again.

The carol singers did more than provide us with an unforget-table evening. Joe, who had seemed to be running on empty, now tapped into a reserve of energy. Knowing that Joy had a small role in a Christmas play at the church, Joe insisted on seeing it. He managed to stay through the first half of the play before asking to be taken home.

Joe's family came for Christmas Day, and he carved the turkey. He even attended a New Year's Eve party given by the friends with whom he had played basketball and softball.

In thinking back to that movie in which the gallant knight had gone on fighting though mortally wounded, the hardest part for me to watch as a child had been when the knight had to take two hands to lift his sword.

Joe had reached the point in his own battle when he could, as it were, no longer lift his sword. Following a night in which he suffered excruciating pain, we all knew (Dad and Mom were with us) that it was time for Joe to leave home and go to the local hospital. Dr. Tony Anthony, our friend, made the decision and the move easier for us.

There was such a richness even about Joe's last days. He and Dad became very close. Joe's parents were often at his bedside, and I was aware of how hard it was for Joe to see the pain in the eyes of his folks.

I was with Dad at Joe's hospital bedside when Joe said with surprising clarity and conviction, "I am not afraid to die. I think you both know that. But how do I free myself from the pain and the guilt of knowing that I could have been a better father, son, and husband?"

Dad said quietly, "There isn't one of us who could not have done things better with our lives." He went on to remind Joe that, at his earlier asking, he had been forgiven and that he could and should now forgive himself.

On the last day in which he was coherent we had our real valedictory moment. His concern, indeed, his only concern, was about our future. He again mentioned a life insurance policy that had been taken out by the Braille School, but uppermost in his mind was where Joy and I were going to live.

I told him that I had given much thought to this question and had decided that we'd go back to California.

"It's best, I think, that we be near my family. So we'll be going back to Bakersfield."

"Good," he whispered, "very good."

"And Joy is excited," I assured him. "She remembers those California vacations."

He said something now that I didn't understand. I bent over the bed, and he interpreted my gesture.

He whispered, "Jay. Keep in touch with Jay."

"We will," I promised. "We'll invite him down for vacations."

"They're both great kids," he whispered.

"Yes, they're great kids."

I was aware of his sudden spasm of pain. For a while we were silent, simply holding hands. Then he turned my hands over and said, "Your hands have worked so hard for me." They were not the last words he spoke to me, but the last words that I understood.

Joe died at four minutes after the midnight of his thirty-sixth birthday. They called me from the hospital. Dad accompanied me to the hospital, where we had a prayer together at Joe's bedside. I reached out and touched Joe's still warm hand. Not being able to see him, I felt the need to do this.

I phoned Jay's mother, who was compassionate and helpful. We agreed it was best that she should give the news to Jay. What I was dreading was having to tell Joy, as soon as she awoke, that her beloved Daddy had gone. She barely stirred when, at dawn, I got into her bed and snuggled with her.

When she eventually awakened she said immediately and calmly, "Daddy's died, hasn't he?"

"Yes," I told her, "very peacefully."

I reached out to stroke her cheeks and, to my surprise, found them to be dry.

"It's okay, Mom," she said quietly, "I've cried all my tears."

There were other times in the next stressful days and weeks when Joy was comforting me. Over and again I asked myself if my daughter was really only eight!

Ten days or so later, and after Mom and Dad had returned to California, I awakened from an unforgettable dream. I had dreamt that Joy and I were holding hands and facing a darkly shadowed mountain. An illuminated pathway traversed the forested lowlands and then soared through the rocky upper slopes. The sun of the new dawning had not yet risen above the mountain's burnished crest.

Strangely, I was not daunted but was comforted, indeed exhilarated, by this dream, for it seemed to hold a promise of good things to come, so long as we held the faith and had the courage to strive and to climb on. Perhaps we could even reach that burnished ridge and thus survey the sun-warmed, illuminated land beyond.

12

Westward Ho!

§

Just as I had mourned the loss of my sight—which, in a way, is another kind of death—so I now mourned the loss of Joe. I experienced, too, as does everyone who loses a loved one, pangs of guilt. Why had I, with my damaged body, survived, and yet Joe, so healthy, so strong, had succumbed?

I was no less vulnerable to negative thinking than any other new widow. How often I was obliged to raise my defensive shield of faith when thinking about the future. Would there be enough money? What about health insurance now that neither Joy nor I were any longer covered by Joe's policy? How to do the shopping? How to be—as I fully intended that we should be— genuinely independent? Now that there was no man to defend us, what about personal security? What if a robber, a rapist . . . ? Up went my shield. Enough, enough!

The evening after the Vinton funeral—a deeply moving rite attended, by among so many others, Joe's Braille School kids—I went downstairs and curled up in Joe's recliner. There, wide awake, I persuaded myself, just momentarily, that Joe was not dead.

It was a scary moment because I recognized how a mind under great stress can slither from reality to psychotic illusion. In the Yankton mental institution I had become familiar with minds that had wandered into schizophrenic wildernesses and had failed to return.

Shocked by where my mind was heading, I sat bolt upright in the chair. I told myself that I was absolutely not going to go crazy.

There were, of course, inconsequential moments when I quite forgot that Joe was not around. The first of these incidents occurred when I was about to take a bath and could not find the drain plug. Loudly, I called out for Joe to come and help me. Then I bit my lower lip until I tasted blood. I managed to plug the tub quite effectively with a washcloth.

I needed therapy. I found it, not on a leather couch, not in the office of a psychologist. I started to write down, in detail, all the experiences I had gone through in the past six years. This writing would be my catharsis and was to prove a powerful therapy. It was also to become the raw material for this book.

To allow me to write, I used a Visual Tek, loaned to me by the Braille School. This instrument is a type of closed-circuit television designed and constructed especially for the partially sighted. The Visual Tek screen magnifies print forty times. The magnification allowed me, with my peripheral vision, to read printed letters—and thus words, one at a time. I was able, for instance, to read on the screen the figures on my phone and electricity bills. Then, by placing my checkbook on the plate below the screen, I could write the figures and my signature on the check. The whole process of paying a bill initially took as long as twenty minutes. But I could do it myself!

I could not accurately read cursive writing, which, when thrown onto the screen, appeared like a string of loops. But with my nose pressed to the screen I could see, as a series of dots, the highly magnified lines in a child's exercise book. When I hand-wrote anything on lined paper, the Visual Tek screen showed me that I was keeping to the lines. The point of my pen appeared to me on the screen as a moving blob.

Writing with the aid of the Visual Tek required all the patience I could muster. I spent hours hunched over the apparatus. The more I used it the better my writing became.

Harnessing the tiny, foggy window of my peripheral vision to this marvelous invention gave me another and critical gateway to the illuminated world. Thus, I first recorded the story of Joy's pink socks. Thus I recorded my feelings when told by Dr. Corbett that I would be blind for the rest of my life. Thus, over months and months—eventually moving into years—I was able to record all the events leading up to and beyond Joe's gallant struggle for life.

Another reason I was able to move purposefully through very difficult times following Joe's death was because we had a new beacon in front of us. More accurately, it was a signpost, and it read "California." I began to chip away at all the decisions that needed to be made in order to get to California. Back and forth went the telephoned dialogues. I began with the same worn phrase: "My husband has just died of cancer and . . . "

Eventually, after meeting with Braille School business officers and with the help of the superintendent, the insurance figures were given to me. Financially I was going to be okay—if, as one adviser cautioned, I were careful, whatever that word meant.

Then came the toughest tasks. What to do with all Joe's papers, clothes, tools, bicycle? Then what about our car, bought new only nine months earlier?

I really loved this car. I'd often rest from other wearying chores, go out to the car, and just sit in it. Sometimes I'd start the engine, rev it up, and press the buttons to move the electric windows up and down. I longed to shift the car into gear and move it, if only for a few yards down the driveway.

Perhaps only an alcoholic thirsting for a bottle could understand my yearning to drive the car somewhere, anywhere, away from this house where I'd shed so many tears, experienced so much pain. Oh, if only I could have my sight back for just one day, an hour, even a few minutes! Thus I mused as I agonized over getting rid of a car I couldn't drive!

It was also hard for me to handle Joe's bicycle. How he'd loved that bike. He'd taken it camping, taken it to the mountains. Joe's hunting gun would go to Jay.

With each touch of clothing, furniture, whatever, a decision was now made. This item would be packed and taken with us. This furniture would be sold. These clothes would be given away.

Joy made her own decisions. She decided to give almost all of her toys, mostly stuffed animals collected from her early childhood, to the little kids in the Braille School dorms. She knew and had befriended many of them. She picked out specific animals for specific children. Then she personally handed them over to the kids of her choice.

"Oh, Mom," she exulted, "it made me feel so warm inside."

I hugged my generous daughter. Then we set about filling

her little red wagon with clothes, all washed and pressed, of course: a mix of Joe's clothes, Joy's clothes, and my own. These we hauled to the Braille School where they were distributed to the neediest children.

Through advertisements in the local newspaper, a yard sale, and a consolidated auction, our possessions were pared down to a few pieces of furniture and a few crates that could be economically transported across most of the continent.

To allow Joy to complete her second grade schooling, we remained in Vinton until the end of May. As soon as she came back from school each day, Joy got down to the business of sorting and packing. We barely stopped for meals. Preparation of meals presented no problem because the freezer was full of food, much of it cooked by friends. However, Joy did promise herself that, once in California, she wouldn't eat ham again until she was a teenager! Ham was the easiest meat for me to serve.

I could have saved a lot of energy agonizing over the disposal of the car. Dad bought it. His own car, he told me on the phone, had reached retirement age. The Blue Book was consulted and the deal made in a couple of minutes. My parents would fly out to Iowa, hand over their return tickets to Joy and to me, and then he and Mom would spend a leisurely four days driving back to California.

It was a perfect solution, as I told Dad after he assured me that the car to which I was so attached would be the car that would be meeting us at Los Angeles airport.

"And you'll promise to drive us to our new home," I insisted.

"Our new home?" queried Joy, who'd been listening to the phone call. I could almost see her elevated eyebrows. "Why didn't you tell me you'd bought a house?"

"I haven't," I told her. "Not yet, but we will. I'm dreaming about it."

Joy slid down from the packing case upon which she'd been sitting and stood in front of me. I was sitting on another crate. She said, "Please, Mom, let me look at the house before you buy it."

I reassured her that I wouldn't consider purchasing a house without her first checking it out. "Your eyes are my eyes," I reminded her.

She leaned into me, her arms around my waist. "Oh, Mom," she said. "It's sometimes hard to be your eyes."

"I know," I told her, "but you're doing beautifully."

"Am I?"

"You're a gift straight from heaven."

I moved my hands up to her shoulder blades, and she asked me what I was doing.

"Feeling for feathers," I told her.

"Feathers?"

"Aren't wings made from feathers?"

Both of us giggled. It was a brief and joyous interlude before we resumed the tiresome labor of sorting and packing.

It was a few days short of three months after Joe's death that the movers arrived. The crates contained dishes, pots and pans, bedding, and the personal things that we'd need for setting up house in Bakersfield.

The only spot in the empty house that provoked any feelings of nostalgia was the second-floor balcony where I stood alone for a few minutes listening to the birds. On cue, the mourning dove sang a few sad notes. Empty, curtainless rooms echoed my footsteps. I deliberately shut down my mind on remembrances, the bright and sparkling ones, the sorrowful ones. There'd be time enough later to recall time's passage here.

The moving van arrived on the same day my parents arrived to pick up the car. They handed over their return tickets to Los Angeles and set off almost immediately for the four-day road journey home.

With us through much of the time that we'd spent preparing for our departure were four women who would, I knew, be life-time friends. They were Cathy Hummel, Deb Englehart, Deb Wilberg, and Brenda Armstrong. For years we had relished each other's company and had shared confidences; our husbands had partied and had played sports together. We had gone to church together, raised children together, wept and laughed together. They had taken Joy in when Joe was sick and when I had lost my sight. They had shopped for me, cooked for me, cleaned house for me, and prayed with me.

All else but these dear friends I could leave behind without heartache. Cathy took Joy and me to her home. We'd stay with her for the next week to give plenty of time for the moving van to reach Bakersfield and for my parents to drive nearly two thousand miles. There was also one other visit that I felt obliged to make. I'd promised Dr. Corbett that I'd see him again before leaving the state.

Cathy drove me to the University of Iowa Hospital, but even as she parked the car I found myself very reluctant to re-enter a building within which such traumatic events had occurred. As we pushed open the hospital's doors my nostrils were assailed again by the unique odor that I had come to hate because it triggered such frightening memories.

Dr. Corbett received me as if I were a VIP. He expressed his sympathy over the loss of Joe and listened attentively as I briefly told him of Joe's courage. I illustrated my report with the story of the carol singers. He then told me how he and his colleagues were still researching the ailment that had deprived me of vision. He had already arranged for my medical file to be transferred to the Department of Ophthalmology at the University of California at Davis. A Dr. John Keltner, a professor of ophthalmology and neurology, would be in charge of my case.

"Very sound man," said Dr. Corbett, "and I'll be keeping in touch with him."

As I stood up, he came around his desk and held my hand in both his. For a few moments the eminent physician seemed at a loss for words. Then he said simply, "I will not forget you, Joan—ever."

I almost hugged him, for I knew he had given me the very best of his skills, and I knew that it had really pained him when he had been obliged to tell me that I would not see again. However, I thought that a hug might have embarrassed him, and perhaps been a breach of medical etiquette.

In a nearby surgical office more blood was drawn from my arm for a final test asked for by Dr. Corbett. Then I told Cathy that there was a nurse I wanted her to meet and that her name was Katy.

"If we're lucky," I said, "we'll find her at a nurses' station in the neurology wing. We'll take elevator F to the second floor, and then take a left."

Cathy was properly impressed when I became her guide, and she laughed when I told her, "I could find my way around this hospital even if I were blindfolded."

We were lucky. Katy walked right into us. We hugged and kissed. I introduced my dearest Vinton friend to my favorite nurse.

Then Katy astounded me by saying to Cathy, "You, too, look like a practicing Christian."

After I had gasped I asked, "Since when did agnostic Katy become a reader of souls?"

Katy laughed infectiously. "Joan will tell you I was as bitter as gall over my messed-up marriage. It's okay, I've forgiven him even though he's still a jerk." Another laugh. "Not sure whether some of my new friends would approve of my calling anyone a jerk—even when he is one. Joan will give you the first two reels of my story. Vegas setting. Blackjack and booze. Joan's partly responsible for the change—my forgiving him for what he did to me. I'm going to—"

I interjected, "That's such nonsense, Katy. It was you who saved my sanity." I turned to Cathy. "When I was here she read my letters aloud—including letters from the blind kids. We soaked each other with our tears."

Katy's cheek was against mine once more. "I'm so terribly sorry about your Joe, honey. Just remember when you're lying under one of those California palm trees that I'm thinking of you—like every day."

"Stop making me cry," I protested.

It was too brief a time with Katy, as it always is with friends of the heart.

Then came the day of our departure. Joe's parents came down from South Dakota to see us off. They drove us to the Cedar Rapids airport. For me there was, of course, no opportunity for last looks at the tree-lined avenues, the familiar stores, or the handsome red-bricked civic buildings. My only recollection of this last drive through pretty Vinton was the whistle of a train and the scent of lilacs.

While on the way to Cedar Rapids, I did allow my mind to survey the more significant Iowa milestones—my arrival here as a bride, starting my work with the blind children I had grown to love, Joy's birth in the local hospital, the day when my eyesight began to fade and fail, and Joe's dying . . .

Alongside me, Joy was obviously unfazed by nostalgic thoughts. "Oh, Mom," she cried, "can we go to the beach real soon?"

I replied, "First we've got to find a new home. And you promised to help me, remember?"

"Oh yes," said Joy, "I forgot. But I just can't wait to get to a beach."

I reminded her that we'd be staying with her California grandparents, possibly for quite a while, as we scouted Bakersfield for "just the right place."

Just before we boarded the airplane there was one more tearful farewell when Joe's parents embraced us. Joe's father, Ken, was holding me when he said, "If there's anything, anything at all that you need or anything we can do for you, please promise to get in touch with us."

I thankfully gave him my promise.

Ninety minutes after leaving Vinton, Joy and I were seated in an airplane thundering down a runway. As the wheels left the ground and the plane soared, a new and extraordinary feeling overwhelmed me. It was a sudden sense of lightness of spirit. No, it was more than that. It was as if I'd left behind a crushing burden. I felt, or so it seemed, the need to rub sore shoulders, to straighten my back (which was still pressed against the seat by the angle of flight and the thrust of the jet engines).

Enshrouded though my eyes were by a veil of darkness, I became deeply conscious of space—space for breathing deeply, for movement, for adventure.

"What do you see through the window?" I asked Joy as the airplane leveled out.

"Just sky," she said.

"You can't see the ground?"

"No, there are clouds covering the ground." She paused and then added, "It's funny, isn't it? Only we can see the blue sky and the sunshine." She corrected herself. "I mean I can see it. But I see it for you, Mom, don't I?"

"Well, today I sort of see it too," I said.

I wasn't sure she understood. But I was learning that Joy, who'd been obliged to mature so quickly, was understanding a lot more than I too often gave her credit for.

She squeezed my hand and said, "I'm so excited, Mom."

"Me too," I said. "Me too."

13

Letters to Cathy

§

On July 4, 1989, I audiotaped this letter to Cathy Hummel in Vinton.

. . . I'm lying in my swimsuit on the enclosed patio of my very own home! Water's tinkling and splashing from a nearby fountain in a manmade lake across the street. Whirr of wings from hummingbird feeder hanging from beam above my head. Temperature in low nineties. Humidity zero. Have your eyes turned green?

My friend Louise—the Basque gal with fiery eyes and emotions to match—found this condominium for us. It's in a new complex, typically Californian—tree-lined avenues, several swimming pools, tennis courts (within earshot when the wind's from the south, with barbecue grill within smelling distance when wind's in the north), clubhouse, shopping center only a block away, Joy's school not much farther. She's still on summer vacation.

Kissin' cousins and friends moved us into the place in one day. The next morning Joy awakened me and confirmed the choice by declaring, "Mom, doesn't it just feel like home!" It did! It does!

The place was professionally decorated by a friend. She has the kind of flair and taste I approve of. Seafoam green carpet (how do I know?—cause she told me, of course!) and curtains to match. I even had my say about the pictures on the walls. I'd always loved seascapes. I simply like to know that they're there.

Cathy, you're one of the few who would understand what happened to me in the first days after we moved in. I spent hours out here on the patio doing nothing at all. The sun enfolded me in a warm blanket. I let my mind drain itself of all emotions.

Been thinking a lot about Joe. There were times when Joe could have been a lot gentler with me. I can see now that what he did was push me so that I could be independent. His attitude strengthened me. Perhaps that is what he was trying to do. Perhaps he had a premonition of his death and he saw that I had to be toughened. We love people when they treat us like kittens and stroke us. We resent it when they kick our butts, as Joe would have phrased it. The kickers are the ones who get us moving.

I'm meandering, Cathy, as I often do when I audiotape letters. Anyway, in the first week in my new home I did almost nothing except allow the past to sort of drift away and then tilt my chin to embrace the future, whatever it is, wherever it takes me.

Thank God for the insurance money, which paid for our home, and I've splurged on a few things, the most important of which is a Visual Tek closed-circuit TV, which cost me $2,500 and is worth every cent! It gives me a critical peephole to the sighted world. I'm also continuing the therapy of writing down the story of the Vinton years. I believe reliving the darkest times (literally, mentally and spiritually) is contributing to a process of self-healing. In the long term the V-Tek will prove a lot more economical than a shrink!

In your letter, Cathy, you asked about our security. You've been reading too many stories about crime in California. This is not LA or the Bay Area and we're still pretty law-abiding here. We've attached bells to the gate facing the street, so I'm always given warning when someone is approaching the front door. I don't open it to strangers unless they can identify themselves as messengers—UPS guys et al.

You ask about my health. Mostly feeling pretty good. Not yet ready to run a marathon, but I am swimming in the pool with Joy, who is developing into a really good swimmer. I've so often bumped my head on the tiled sides of the pool that I'm ready to patent edge-side cushions like the ones on a pool table. Also, I've been to Davis to see the chief ophthalmologist at the university, a Dr. John Keltner, who is now in charge of my case. He seems to be no less intrigued than was Dr. Corbett. Liked him a lot—quiet, caring, competent.

What else, Cathy, my dear? I'm trying to be good. Sometimes have some confusing thoughts, especially when a strong arm tugs me out of the pool and a vibrant male voice invites me to a barbecue!

Love to you and Dennis—also to the two Debs and to Brenda. Blow kisses to everyone I know in that little town with a big heart.

Joan

Letters were so very important to me. I became quite frustrated when Joy was not around to collect the mail from our box—one of about thirty boxes placed some two hundred yards from my front door. It was Joy who decided that it was time for me to collect the mail myself. She marked out the route to the mailboxes by helping me to feel two fire hydrants, with my cane pacing out the sidewalk to an appropriate right turn, listening to the sound of another fountain, picking up the fuzzy shadows of some trees where I needed to cross a street, feeling a V-shaped slice in the curb, and so on.

I was getting quite cocky about my mobility, but that old caution about pride heralding a fall is no less applicable to someone carrying a white cane. What my cane did not tell me one morning was that a gardener had parked his truck within a stone's throw of the mailboxes, and that the steel handle of his Weed Eater was sticking out over the sidewalk.

The blow across the bridge of my nose and forehead threw me to the ground. I was so dazed and bewildered that I had no idea where I was. I'd quite forgotten the important count of paces from the last corner. I didn't even know what had hit me. Indeed, my first thought was that I'd been mugged. Farther along the street I could hear gardeners mowing a lawn. I somehow managed to find my way back home.

The bruises and the cut healed well, but the accident was a setback to my self-esteem.

Neighbors soon learned that the new owner of number sixty-two was a bit crazy. When frustrated by misplacing the house keys, for example, or discovering that Joy had failed to replace the milk container in the refrigerator, I usually screamed into a pillow. But I suspected that the neighbors sometimes heard me. I could almost hear them sighing, "Ah, well, there she goes once more—probably misplaced the Scotch tape this time."

November 7, 1989. A letter audiotaped to Cathy Hummel in Vinton:

> . . . So you scold me for not "doing anything." But I am, and it's exciting. I've just signed up for a speech class at the junior college here. I met a fabulous professor, Dr. Chuck Wall, who's blind but has four master's degrees and a doctorate in business. Anyway, Chuck asked me to help him with a class of blind people. My first

reaction was negative. I felt I'd given enough years to teaching the blind. But I changed my mind when he told me that in this class-room was the latest model of a talking computer. They had talking computers at the Braille School, but I never learned how to use them. This incredible machine actually talks back to you in a robot voice. It tells you what you've typed.

However, I wondered whether there was any purpose in my learning how to use this sophisticated machine because I could never afford to buy one. It costs an arm and a leg.

But then a miracle! We're told to expect miracles every day, aren't we? We've had so many, but this one was major league.

It all began with a terrible tragedy about fifteen years ago when three twenty-one-year-old girls were killed on a street here in Bakersfield. One of the girls was Maria, the daughter of a Dutch family who were members of my dad's church. Maria was one of my closest friends. I was a student in South Dakota when Maria and the two other girls were walking away from a restaurant and a car plowed into them. Maria was killed instantly, and her two friends died shortly after the three girls had been mowed down. Mom phoned me with the news of this tragedy, which was big headlines here. I remember so well how I walked across to the col-lege chapel in Vermillion. I prayed and wept alone for an hour, perhaps two hours, I can't be sure.

Well, as I said, all this happened a long time ago. Then, three Sundays back, after church here, Maria's parents, Leonard and Margaret Van Doorn, came up to me and said they had heard I was interested in a talking computer.

Mr. Van Doorn, who still has a very strong Dutch accent, said, "Ve, my vife and me, vould like much to give you a talking com-puter." Mrs. Van Doorn said, "Yes, ve like to do that."

I was just bowled over. I told them that they couldn't possibly know what these computers cost and I couldn't accept such an extravagant gift. We're talking about thousands of dollars.

Mr. Van Doorn took my arm and said, "Now, you lizzen good, Joan. God has blessed us. Ve can do no more for our Maria, zo you let us do thiz for you, yez?" He added that their friends and my family's friends, Ron and Nedra Lehr—also farmers—wanted to come in on this incredible gift.

Hugs! Kisses! Tears! Wonderment! So I have this absolutely incredible talking computer at my home. I'm taking lessons at the college on how to operate it, and I hope to be able to help other blind students use it.

Am enjoying a speech class, too. Mom, who's taking an art class at the junior college, drives me there. The other twenty-five people in the class seem to be intrigued to have a blind woman learning about voice and diction. I always sit at the end of the second row from the front. Sometimes I'm late, but they always leave this desk for me.

After about five sessions, the professor asked us all to talk about ourselves for three minutes. Most of my classmates are hoping to become radio announcers. There're some from overseas hoping to improve their communication skills.

Boy, oh boy! Which experience should I bowl them over with?

The others in the class were to be allowed to read their speeches. I was going to have to remember mine. I gave the mini-speech a lot of thought. Then I recalled an experience shared with Joy a few weeks earlier. I typed out the speech on my talking computer, which played it back to me several times until it was memorized, more or less.

I could sense some tension among my classmates when it was my turn to speak. Most of them had tended to avoid me, perhaps assuming that since I'm blind I'm also half-witted. I found the podium quite easily. Believe you might be interested in what I said. Here it is:

"Good afternoon.

"I'm going to talk about a recent experience at Pismo Beach. When my nine-year-old daughter, Joy, and I walked the beach barefooted, she pounced on shells and told me about their colors and their shapes. It was quite cool that early morning, with eddies of fog coming in from the sea—so Joy told me. It is nice for me to walk in the surf because I love the feel of sand between my toes and I can count on there being nothing to bump into. We reached the wharf, where Joy now gave me a guiding elbow.

"We sat on a splintery wooden bench and listened to the music of the waves. Then the sun came through and warmed our faces. It was a gentle time for both of us. Joy felt close and comfortable enough to speak of something that was troubling her.

"'Yes?' I said, encouraging her.

"Joy half buried her face in my windbreaker, and said, 'Lots of kids tell me that they feel sorry for me—having a father who died and a blind mother. I hate it when they tell me that.'

"I bent my head until my cheek touched her fog-dampened hair and suggested that other kids were really wanting to be kind. I told her that I didn't like it, either, when people smothered me with sympathy.

"We got up and walked again, her arm still around my waist. I was happy that my small daughter could share these deep feelings with me. What she had told me made me more aware that she, too, was having to deal with difficulties related to my blindness.

"That morning of our walking on Pismo Beach will remain with me, for the passing of this hour of my life contained moments of shared beauty, shared sadness, and shared love."

Cathy, there was such absolute silence in the room following this mini-speech that I wondered whether I had bored my classmates or embarrassed them. Then someone at the back of the classroom clapped, then they all applauded. I smiled, but I had to pretend to look at my shoes as I made my way back to the end seat in the second row from the front. I didn't want them to see my tears.

There's a P.S. to this little cameo of my life down here in California. Most of my classmates have now become my friends.

Dear love to you, Cathy, as always,

Joan

Several months after I had first met the brilliant and blind Professor Chuck Wall, he and his wife, Di, invited Joy and me to spend the weekend in their log cabin in the High Sierras, which was about a two-hour drive from Bakersfield. Only a four-wheel-drive vehicle could get up that steep and winding dirt road.

As we traveled, Chuck told us a little of his life and how, in his late teens, he had had such trouble reading that he'd been labeled retarded. He was diagnosed with retinitis pigmentosa, which inevitably destroys eyesight. What excited him was to know that he wasn't dumb after all. He went on to become a superior scholar and gained his doctorate in business. He recently ran for mayor of Bakersfield, and came in third.

When we reached the cabin, which I think was about 5,000 feet above sea level, the air was like chilled wine and was perfumed by fir trees. The cabin itself was rustic, constructed of logs, with a loft, kitchen, and guest bedroom. Chuck and Di have channeled a small stream just outside, so that its bubbling can lull them to sleep.

While Di and Joy found work to do in the garden and the kitchen, Chuck called me to the balcony where he sat me in one of his homemade rockers.

"Aah," I sighed, "the sounds of silence."

"Silence! You're not listening, my girl," said Chuck.

"You must learn to listen to the song of life. Can't you hear that blue jay over on the left, and that warbling whistle is a mountain bluebird. Then that unmusical fella trilling away on the right is almost certainly a loggerhead shrike."

Chuck had taped scores of birdsongs heard near his cabin, and he is able to name them as accurately as a conductor can pick out any orchestral instrument that's off-key. On this visit, and on later ones, I began to be able to identify the different song birds.

One had the sense that this was Chuck's and Di's mountain, and in their contentment in the high country they were more like teenagers. Their laughter, their love for each other and life, and their high enthusiasm made their cabin so vibrant and exciting.

Since these weekends spent with the Walls, Chuck has become internationally famous from coining the phrase, "Today do a random act of senseless kindness!" He thought up this idea after hearing a radio news story about "another random act of senseless violence." He assigned one of his classes to undertake "a random act of senseless kindness" as a project. The idea really caught on. Now, all across the nation and overseas, people are turning the familiar negative news phrase into a positive personal commitment.

A woman in his class recorded an amusing random act of senseless kindness. She had just parked her car in a full lot when she noticed another car circling for space. The woman backed her car and waved in the circling car. She herself was obliged to park a long distance from the classroom. He told me, too, that a very intrigued Princess Diana had been inquiring about his random-act-of-senseless-kindness project. Many of the volunteers who went to the aid of victims of the recent devastating earthquake in Los Angeles wore T-shirts bearing Chuck's slogan. I believe that the brilliant and ebullient Chuck could run for the U.S. Senate on this slogan alone!

To me and to so many, Chuck is one special guy. He's my sage of the mountains. He always leaves me with an original thought. "Joan," he said to me on one occasion, "remember that those of us who walk in darkness or twilight must turn on our own lights."

Here's an audiotaped letter to Cathy dated November 30, 1991:

> . . . I'm becoming the Merry Widow. Fine with me if you now want to put on Franz Lehar music while you listen to this tape.
>
> Six weeks ago I went to my first dance. Actually, I was dragged to it by my friend, Sandy, who's into country and western. I'd learned the basic steps when I was in high school, but felt sure that I'd forgotten everything.
>
> Well, we'd hardly gotten ourselves into the dance hall when this guy with a Southern accent and cowboy boots (Sandy told me) came up and grabbed my hand. I was trying to tell him that I was here only to listen to the band, but Sandy blurted out that I was "a pro."
>
> Not sure whether this guy thought I'd come from the red light district (if Bakersfield has one!) or whether I'd understudied Juliet Prowse. So Sandy pushed me onto the floor and I pleaded with Mr. Cowboy Whoever not to let go of my hand.

"Trust me," he said. I'd always been taught that when a strange guy says those two words, you don't just walk to the door—you run! Well, I did some trusting as he whirled me around to a familiar beat. Memory clicked into the right groove, and I felt I was performing reasonably well. Then the music stopped and guess what? This cowboy gentleman (huh!) left me in the middle of the dance floor! I think he tossed a "Thank you, ma'am" over his left shoulder.

But now what do I do? I listen for mocking laughter. I heard some and I started walking toward it. Yes, it was Sandy. She told me she was so amused that she had had to run to the bathroom! The good thing I got out of all this was appreciating that Mr. Cowboy Whatever had obviously not realized I was blind! In fact he came back later and asked me to dance again.

Then I've been to a number of parties with new friends, mostly encountered poolside. Tracy and Sheri both have daughters about the same age as Joy.

Dearly beloved Louise, my bestest friend, as Joy would put it, encourages me to continue to write. She takes me shopping for clothes, takes me to spas, takes us to the beach, and she arrives at the house when I most need company.

Once I phoned Louise at three in the morning just to talk! I felt desperately lonely and—well—beaten up and miserably discouraged. How many folks can you call for a chat at that time of night?

But, Cathy, I'm now going to confess something awful and how I risked this wonderful friendship.

It was quite a small incident that caused the near disaster. Joy came rushing and screaming into the house. Eventually she blurted out that she had pinched her thumb on the front gate. A pinched thumb can be darned sore, we all know that. Instead of coming to

me, though, Joy went to Louise, and I heard Louise saying that
she'd help make the thumb better.

Instead of being grateful for Louise's care, I felt resentment and
jealousy. Heck! I thought, aren't I the child's mother? I should be
attending to Joy's hurt. I shouted at my daughter to stop crying and
to let me see her thumb.

"But you can't see, Mom."

Joy's retort stabbed my heart.

Louise said quietly, "It's okay, Joan. There isn't any blood and
she can move it. I'm just going to bathe the thumb under a cold
faucet."

I tugged Joy away from my friend. My voice was high pitched
as I shouted, "Stay out of this, Louise. I can handle it. I'm her
mother. Just you remember that . . . "

Joy was softly crying again. She was obviously upset by my
raised voice. I pulled her to the bathroom. Then I heard the sound
of the front door closing, followed by the sound of Louise's car
starting up and pulling away.

Cathy, I felt sick! I mean, totally nauseated! What on earth had
I done? I knew I'd hurt Louise deeply. Yet I now tried to make
excuses. Wasn't I quite capable of looking after a pinched thumb?
Hadn't I been a lifeguard in my college years? Hadn't I taught
CPR to the staff at the Braille School? What right had Louise to
play mother to my daughter? Why should I call and apologize?
Louise was going to have to call me.

Three days passed and no word from Louise. Four miserable
days passed. On the fifth day I was ready to admit that I'd been an
absolute jackass! Somewhere, not far removed from panic, I began
to wonder whether Louise would ever speak to me again.

What really shook me up, Cathy, was discovering what an
ungrateful witch (spell that with a B!) I could be. Me! Moi!

Who was it who said, "We've all got a potential Hitler and Mother Teresa in us?"

Of course a very, very penitent Joan called the dearest friend of her childhood. Louise had to have dropped anything she was doing, because within record time she was at my home, forgiving me and hugging me. Thank God!

Dearest love,

Joan

In January 1991, I wrote a letter to Cathy on my talking computer. There were a few misspellings. That amazing robot inside the machine that reads back what I've written is not yet the world's best speller! He's completely foxed by words like "kibbutz."

However, here are several paragraphs from my (edited) computer-written letter to Cathy, dated January 1991:

. . . As promised, I'm really getting on with the story of my life. Well into the Vinton years. Amazing that something begun as a thought process when I was in the hospital is now getting into type. I find it so hard to relive some of those days that the tears well up.

Joy sometimes finds me crying while at the machine. She wants to know why I have to write about sad things. I tell her that it is good for me. Difficult to explain the word catharsis to a ten-year-old.

Oh, gosh, Cathy! How I embarrassed her the other day.

I needed a white blouse, so I took Joy along to a department store to help me choose one. Joy went deep into the store to find out where they sold these things. Out of the tiny corner of my eye, which allows me to see light and blobby shapes, I saw what I assumed was a saleslady in a skirt and blazer.

I stopped and said, "I wonder if you can help me? I'm looking for a blouse."

I was going into some detail about the kind of garment I needed when Joy returned and started tugging at my sleeve.

In a horrified stage whisper Joy said, "Mom, you're talking to a mannequin!"

Poor Joy was so embarrassed because a number of nearby shoppers had to have heard the monologue.

Oh, and I must tell you about the Joanmobile. Well, I spoke some time ago at a service club, and afterward one of the members came up to me and said that he built three-wheel bikes—big-wheelers for grown-ups. He asked me if I'd like one.

"How much?" asked the frugal me. "My pleasure," he said. I'd all but forgotten about this offer when, just before Christmas, this guy presents me with what Joy calls her Corvette and what I call my Joanmobile. It's so cool. It has two side-by-side saddles and is powered by four pedals. Under the seats there is a basket for groceries. It's steered by a bar handle.

Naturally Joy is the navigator. She's also the chief pedal-pusher—though she doesn't know this, and so please don't tell her! It's now a breeze to go grocery shopping.

You were amused by my telling you that I'm becoming more and more the Merry Widow. I'm really enjoying socializing. Been to a few more dances with the girls. Then I must tell you about something that happened to me in Sacramento. I traveled up there by Amtrak (they looked after me as if I were royalty, and I wrote to the people at the top to tell them so) to see my ophthalmologist, Dr. Keltner. He asked me if I'd mind answering questions from his medical students. Of course I agreed—same old questions, and same old answers.

After this was over I mentioned to Dr. Keltner that I'd been doing some public speaking. He was intrigued because his department is always needing funds for the expansion of facilities and charitable work. He asked me to meet his chief fund-raiser, Joan Hadley. I soon realized that I was meeting someone of exceptional grace and charm.

I gave several talks in Sacramento—including a Rotary Club speech, a speech to the physicians associated with the university ophthalmology department, and a TV interview—to help raise funds for the Medical Center. I usually stayed overnight at Joan Hadley's lovely home. After one visit, when I'd made a speech that seemed to have been well received, she and another friend, Carrie Lou, decided on the spur of the moment to go to "high tea" in San Francisco's famous St. Francis Hotel. We were like kids playing hookey as we boarded the train for the Bay Area. Our first stop was at Saks Fifth Avenue (where I bought some perfume), our second at fabulous Nordstrom's (live piano music!) where we headed for the fine dresses department.

While I was trying on those beautiful gowns I felt like Cinderella herself. "Where's the pumpkin coach?" I asked my friends, who kidded me that I should be modeling for Yves Saint Laurent. But Cathy, those garments I didn't have the cash to buy did funny things to me. I felt something I'd not felt for a long time. I felt sensuous, feminine.

Write soon. I'm no longer allowing anyone to tell me to feel guilty about—well—about things past. They are past, Cathy. I don't have to remind myself of that every day anymore.

Lots of love from Sexy Sue—also known as Joan.

14

The Theater of My Mind

§

Through Joe's struggle against his mortal disease, through my period of mourning, I'd unconsciously suppressed desires for male companionship. But now, in a crowded mall, or while sitting in a bus or in a restaurant, I was aware of men again. I enjoyed the bracing scent of aftershave. I was conscious of the male touch. If I were introduced to a man with a pleasant laugh or an attractive voice, I found myself holding onto a hand a second or two longer than was required by courtesy. This was not necessarily a flirtatious gesture. It was simply that my sense of touch helped me compensate for my loss of sight.

What I was still having a hard time doing was persuading myself that I was still attractive. Surely, went my foolish thoughts in darker moments, my sightless eyes have lost their sparkle. Surely the experience of watching my robust husband fade and die had left some scars upon my face—not physical ones, but telltale signs bespeaking trials and hurts.

Hadn't I read somewhere that a face presents a map of one's life experiences? If there be validity in this proposition (and I doubt it), did my face now reveal the sorrow and the horror of the recent years? Were friends and kin too timid to tell me that my eyes were sunken and dark-rimmed, my mouth downcast when in repose? I suspected that the devil himself planted these silly but disturbing notions in my mind.

There are very few people who can picture their own faces. Instant recognition in a mirror is obviously no problem, but I've yet to meet anyone who is able to describe him or herself as others see them.

Yet curiously I am able to recall my own mirror-image of the time before I lost my sight. I like what I recall. I see blonde hair lying across my shoulders. I see a nose of—well—quite respectable proportions (ha, ha!), a slightly cleft chin, high cheekbones, and a smile—ah yes, a smile!

I happen to have had the best of all orthodontists—the Creator of All Things, including teeth!

No dentist ever suggested braces; in fact, the one who was responsible for giving me regular checkups throughout my teenage years complained that if all his patients were like me he'd be carrying "Hungry and Homeless" placards down the main street. I can see him now, waving his tiny examining mirror and saying, "Joan, I don't know if you have webbed toes. I don't know if you have birthmarks in unusual places, but I can tell you that you've got absolutely perfect teeth." His nurse and I joined in his laughter.

Since I liked to smile and since I was doing a lot of smiling once again, why did I give any heed to those negative whispers inside my head that hinted I was a close cousin of Cinderella's ugly stepsisters?

But then there was an incident, trifling enough, which did wonders for me. I was taking a walk in the far corner of our condominium complex with an elderly neighbor who was a sometime baby-sitter for Joy. The sounds of saws and hammers indicated that we were passing a building under repair or construction. The banging and buzzing of labor suddenly ceased, and I heard whistles—a whole chorus of wolf whistles!

"Just who are they whistling at?" I asked my friend, whose elbow I was grasping. My first and quite genuine presumption was that a mini-skirted teenager was swaying her hips on the sidewalk somewhere ahead of us.

An explosion of laughter from my companion. "Who do you think, my dear?" she exclaimed. "Certainly not me!"

"You're telling me that . . . "

"Indeed I am," said my friend, drowning my astonishment with more laughter. Then she added, "Perhaps you'd like to sue half a dozen brawny and bare-chested young men for harassment?"

I giggled in disbelief and from embarrassment. By now we had moved some thirty or forty paces beyond the construction site. However, one man continued to whistle. To convince myself that he was really directing his unsubtle salutation to me, I stopped, turned, smiled and waved. My gestures prompted another chorus of whistles—the kind of ear-piercers made by inserting a thumb and middle finger under the tongue.

It was a moment or two before we could continue walking, because laughter almost crippled us. The whistling died only when we had turned a corner; those guys up on the scaffolding had no idea what a boost they had given to my morale.

However, gains in self-esteem these days came from more than wolf whistles. I was receiving an increasing number of invitations to speak to different groups. I'd started with church groups, then I'd received a number of invitations from schools. Now I was getting requests from service clubs and associations of various kinds.

With the help of my talking computer and a tape recorder I worked diligently on refining my talks. Naturally I gave a very different talk to sixth-grade kids than to Rotarians. But the theme was the same. I saw how important it was neither to belittle the difficulties and challenges I had faced nor the problems likely being faced by some people in my audiences; but I was anxious to promote and project my belief that, whatever the challenges, whatever the hurts, life still goes on, grimly at times, but also triumphantly.

Here I'm oversimplifying the theme of my talks. Sometimes I'd speak for an hour. Sometimes I was given only twenty minutes, and I might perhaps be obliged to compete with the rattle of teacups.

Two of my speeches in this period were to have a major impact on my life. By the fall of 1991 word had gotten around Bakersfield and communities not far distant that there was this woman (me!) in the area who had a very unusual personal story to tell and that she knew how to tell it.

But here I must backpedal and speak of my connection with the blind celebrity Tom Sullivan. When I was in college in South Dakota, and later, working at the Braille School, I'd read and reread Tom's best-selling autobiography, *If You Could See What I Hear*. I'd also seen the movie based on his book. I'd seen him on television when he had co-hosted *Good Morning America*, and I'd seen him as a featured actor in half a dozen movies. I knew him to be a composer, performer, athlete—and, as someone once put it, "almost everything else except a brain surgeon." In recent years he'd become one of the most in-demand speakers on the lecture circuit.

For me, and for so many others who are disabled, Tom Sullivan's extraordinary achievements were a tremendous inspiration.

My lawyer brother, Jon, was in the audience when Tom spoke to a convention of business people in Bakersfield. Jon is not given to using superlatives, but he pulled out all the stops when he spoke to me about Tom's lecture. I was asked by another member of Jon's legal firm, a man who knew about my own modest lectures, if I'd be interested in getting in touch with Tom. Phone calls were made, and a few mornings later I found myself speaking to Tom on the phone.

This first call—now one of scores from and to Tom Sullivan—lasted ninety minutes! What amazed me about this man, who was to become such a dear and influential friend, was that he was so unhurried. He was genuinely intrigued by my own story. This man, who was honored by the high and the mighty and, as I was later to learn, by the lowliest and the suffering, asked penetrating questions about my difficulties, questions that no one else had thought to ask me.

I told him about my hopes of writing a book and of my daring to hope that I, too, could become an inspirational speaker. He promised to help me with both aspirations.

He said, "Joan, there are tens of thousands, hundreds of thousands, who are waiting to be given a lift by the story that only you can tell."

"Only me?" I queried.

"Only you," repeated Tom, "because all of us are absolutely unique."

This phrase was branded into my mind.

Tom went on to tell me of some of the people he had been able to touch with his own story and activities. One special focus of his interest has been children—blind and otherwise disabled children. He'd raised a great deal of money for a school for blind children, and I was fascinated to learn how he and others were helping disabled children to ski in Colorado.

"Kids who have lost limbs, kids with cancer—we bring them in from all parts of the country and get them on the slopes. They revel in the snow, in sledding and skiing. They forget they're crippled. They forget they're meant to be dying. They start living again—tasting every drop in the cup, even when, as with some of them, the cup of life is almost drained."

"But you surely don't ski yourself?" I asked.

"I surely do," he replied, "and everyone gets out of the way when they see two skiers coming down the slope, one wearing a placard reading 'BLIND SKIER' and the other wearing a placard reading 'BLIND GUIDE'!"

Tom's open-throated laughter was so infectious my eyes were streaming.

"Well, Joan, we're going to have to get you moving," said Tom, "and one good place to start under the big tents is at the Million Dollar Round Table."

"I've no idea what you're talking about," I told him.

"It's an annual convention of high-powered, international business executives. They're always on the hunt for new and effective speakers."

"Are you talking about me, Tom?"

"Is there anyone else on this line? Joan, you've got to learn to lift your eyes to the far horizons."

"But my eyes don't work, Tom. Did I forget to tell you?"

"I'm speaking about the vision of your potential and creative ambition and your guts," said Tom. This time he wasn't laughing.

I'm tempted to speak here at greater length about this memorable phone conversation, which left me with a pounding heart. But we'll be meeting Tom again before my story is finished.

Before I did this backpedaling to bring in my link to Tom Sullivan, I referred to two of my speeches that had a far-reaching impact on my life. The first of these was to a Bakersfield Rotary Club luncheon meeting. Much as an actor becomes aware of and responds to positive feedback in a theater, so I could now gauge an audience's positive response, even when, as so often happened at luncheon get-togethers, waiters or waitresses were still busying themselves with dessert plates or coffee cups.

I still don't know what it is that triggers total attention or gives an almost electric charge to ambience, but I did know on this occasion that the Rotarians were listening—I mean, really listening. Some of the members knew my parents and my brother's family. More than one had been in school with me, and perhaps they were amazed that I could get up on my hind legs in front of a large group and say something of interest.

A few days after the Rotary luncheon, I received a call from one of the club's members, Mr. Richard Sullenger, who, after introducing himself, said he had been out of town and had missed my speech.

"But I'm told," he continued, "that I missed the best speech the club's had in a very long while."

"Oh," I responded with genuine surprise. "Why, thank you, and how nice of you to phone me."

Then Mr. Sullenger astonished me by asking if I'd ever heard of the Million Dollar Round Table. He must have marked my intake of breath, because he added, "Sounds as if you know about it."

I then told him about my recent conversation with Tom Sullivan, whom Mr. Sullenger had heard speak on two occasions. He raved about Tom.

Mr. Sullenger went on, "It happens that I'm not only a member of the Million Dollar Round Table, but I'm also on the committee of ten that picks the speakers for the annual conventions. Now, Joan, I have two questions for you, and if you give a yes to each of them I'd like to try to get you on the platform for the 1993 Million Dollar Round Table in Boston. First, have you got an audio or, preferably, a videotape of one of your lectures? And second, do you think you could muster the courage to speak to an audience of five thousand?"

After a deep swallow, I replied as nonchalantly as though such questions were tossed at me every day, "Yes and yes."

The summer of '93 was still a long way ahead, so after returning the phone to its cradle, I told myself in words close to those used by Scarlett O'Hara, "Fiddle-dee-dee, I'll think about that in about eighteen months."

Then I returned to my talking computer and continued to work on a forty-minute speech I'd been asked to give to a Bakersfield high school on the Thursday before the Christmas break. This task was good for me, if only because it helped to keep the size of my hat unchanged!

When that date came around, I found myself in a gymnasium setting. The kids had listened attentively and had applauded warmly. It was now question time. A girl's voice came down to me from halfway up the bleachers.

"Mrs. Beringer, it's still very hard to even imagine what it's like to be blind. I think I'd just want to die if I lost my sight. I'm wondering, though, what you miss the most."

My first thought was to feel sorry and guilty that I'd left the girl—and perhaps others in the audience—feeling depressed. Certainly I had spoken about the sadder times of my life. In so doing I'd been aware of the collective sorrow, even discomfort. But before concluding this talk I'd gotten the youthful audience to laugh. They'd particularly enjoyed the story of how Joy had once found me engaged in a monologue with a store mannequin.

It was never my intention to "play the audience." I'd been taken aback at one service club where the emcee had boomed heartily, "Joan, you sure know how to press the right buttons."

To me, a "button-presser" sounded as slickly professional as a stand-up comedian. The last reaction I ever sought was an audience of any makeup leaving a hall, a gymnasium, or luncheon tables with tightened jaws or dabbing their eyes.

However, the girl's question caught me off guard. Curiously, I'd never before been asked what she now wanted to know.

"What do I miss most?" I repeated the query, playing for a few seconds of time. My mind scanned for a credible answer.

"Obviously there are a number of things I miss very much," I said blithely. "I miss seeing my daughter's face as she begins—as many of you in this room now begin—to grow from childhood to young womanhood. Yes, I do miss seeing blue skies and the fresh green of springtime. Oh, gosh! I do miss driving a car and the independence that driving a car would allow me. I miss—oh, I suppose my list is a long one, and I guess the school bell is about to ring for your next classes. But if you speak to me of sunsets, or calico cats, or baseball homers my imagination shifts into high gear.

"Every day I thank God for memory and for the gift of imagination. I believe that sometimes the pictures I see in my mind's eye are likely to be more vivid than yours, more beautiful, funnier perhaps, or sadder. I believe that—"

My long response to a simple question was drowned by the shrill sound of the school bell. The high school students stirred.

The school's principal approached and took the microphone from my hand. Above a continuing clatter from the bleachers he said some kind words that evoked more polite applause. The principal managed to squeeze in a couple of announcements—something about a changed time slot for the school band practice, and how an English teacher wanted her tenth grade class to go straight to the library . . .

While I waited for a guiding arm, that final question from the bleachers began to haunt me. It stayed with me all through the lunch with the faculty. It continued to prod and jab during the long drive home chauffeured by a chattering member of the PTA. It still floated around when an effervescent (usually effervescent) Joy returned home from her own school. The question returned to haunt me when I went to bed. It held sleep at bay until the small hours.

What did I really miss most? All along I had known the answer but had avoided phrasing it.

I missed a man. I missed a lover's fingers stroking my hair. I missed a male shoulder upon which to rest my head. I missed whispers in the dark, dialogue at the breakfast table. I missed a male voice telling me that I looked pretty, or promising to fix the vacuum cleaner when he returned from the office.

I missed cooking him a T-bone steak, knowing he liked it medium-rare. I missed dancing with him cheek to cheek at a local nightspot or, less elegantly, on the living room carpet. I missed guileless male laughter when I made a fool of myself.

It was not, of course, the first time I had thought about how nice it would be to get married again—little heart stabs felt most often when I was with friends who were happily married. But

I'd not permitted myself to brood or pine on these occasions.

However, the girl who had asked the question from the gymnasium bleachers had put a match to a fuse, and the fuse was hissing away in my head. I was nervous about it, because I knew it could lead to a barrel of explosive self-pity.

The small hours of the morning (I'd heard the chimes of the mantelpiece clock in the living room sound off the hours) are not the easiest of times to curb covetousness and deep yearnings.

As I now recall that wakeful night I feel my cheeks flaming from embarrassment over confessing that a reasonably well-educated woman who was in her thirties could conceive of herself as being the heroine of a Gothic novel. This was more or less the direction that my thoughts had taken me. Before I took myself in hand, all that my imagination needed was a very small nudge to create a lurid, paperback cover—to see myself with a ripped white blouse, an Adonis pulling me to his saddle and, for good measure, a blazing mansion in the distance!

Later—and in this instance much later—it is easy to laugh at this fantasy and folly. But there it was, all the same, this fresh interest in finding a mate and in creating a two-parent family once again.

When I thumped my pillows for the fourteenth time, there was no recognizable man upon the stage of my mind. Would I have slept at all that night had I known that he was standing in the wings?

15

The Butterfly Man

§

There are quite a few unwritten rules for those who have lost their sight. One of them is that, when taking a shower, you don't drop the soap. Among the blind students at the Bakersfield college is one who claims to be applying for an entry in *The Guinness Book of Records* because he spent seven and a half minutes groveling on the white tiles of his bathroom looking for the soap that had slipped through his hands!

On a morning between Christmas and New Year's I broke the soap-dropping rule. I was on my knees in the shower, and thus a fig leaf more naked than Eve, when the bedroom telephone rang imperiously. Realizing now that the answering machine wasn't on, I uttered a naughty word. Then, after dripping water across the bedroom carpet, I picked up the phone.

"Yup?" I said, still seething.

An unfamiliar male voice responded, "Sorry—must be the wrong number."

"Who do you want?" I demanded.

"Joan Beringer," said the voice.

"You've got her," I said, "but if you're selling . . ."

"Sure doesn't sound like you," said the voice.

"Caught me in a bad moment," I apologized. "You see, I lost the soap in the shower."

"You what?"

My frustration had cooled. "It's just that, well, forget it. Who's speaking?"

It was Scott Clare. He'd been in high school with me. He was now a teacher himself and only a few weeks earlier had invited me to speak to the kids at his school. He was phoning, he said, to invite me to his fortieth birthday party.

"Imagine it, Joan, I'm cresting the hill in a couple of days. I need you at the wake."

"The wake?"

"I'm halfway to eighty!" he moaned. "It's okay. You don't have to wear black."

Scott, who'd been named the funniest guy in our graduating class, clarified the invitation. His wife, Diane, was giving him a surprise party. He'd been instructed to invite his friends and then told to forget whom he'd invited.

I was trying to keep up with Scott's convoluted thought process and, at the same time, trying to dry myself off with a T-shirt I'd previously draped across the bed.

He continued, "There'll be a few people you'll know, but, obedient to Diane's instructions, I've already forgotten their names."

"Scott, is your domestic life always so complicated?" Both of us chuckled. "Anyway, I do have one problem. Isn't your place about five miles from here, on the other side of town?"

"Give or take a few hundred yards," he said.

"Well, for some reason, the DMV won't give me a driving license."

A guffaw from Scott. Then, "Problem solved," he said. "I'll pick you up myself. In any event, Diane wants me out of the house to give her time to blow up balloons and put little sausages on toothpicks, that sort of thing. I'll be at your place at six. Real informal. Okay?"

"Okay," I said enthusiastically.

I was now enjoying parties. There had been two or three occasions when I'd been caught among strangers who were obviously uncomfortable with a blind person. Those of us who've lost our sight have been so stereotyped that it is assumed by some that we are half-witted or that we carry some deadly bug.

Joy gave me every encouragement to get out and about because she enjoyed her sitters and could watch her favorite TV programs without protests from her mother. For formal occasions Joy liked to have some say in what would be suitable to wear. "No, not that yellow dress, Mom. It needs a safety pin to keep your bra strap from showing . . . "

For Scott's party I chose a pair of jeans and a peasant blouse. Joy approved, but reached for the Q-tips. "Too much mascara, Mom," she said, "and you've got some lipstick on your teeth." This from an eleven-year-old!

The sitter arrived on time and was warmly greeted. Annie was asked by Joy whether she thought my earrings were too small. Annie tactfully hemmed and hawed.

"No, Mom," said Joy firmly, "not those with that blouse. You should be wearing gypsy earrings."

I humored my daughter. I usually did. She selected gypsy earrings and danced with me around the carpet. The three of us were laughing when Scott rang the doorbell. He said he could hear the sounds of ribald laughter halfway down our street.

He added mournfully, "I'd hoped for condolences on this milestone occasion."

"Are you fifty or sixty today?" asked a laughing Joy.

Scott drawled, "How can such a beautiful woman produce a daughter who teases me like that?"

"Yes, Mom is beautiful, isn't she?" said Joy. "And I'm so glad that I look like her."

I turned away. Oh, Joy! Oh, my Joy! I thought. How dark and empty my life would be without you.

In danger of smudging mascara, I mumbled some excuse and went to the bedroom. There I pressed my palms into the edge of the dresser until I felt in charge of my emotions again. Then I firmly resolved that were I ever to marry again, the man would have to love my daughter at least half as much as I loved her right now.

When we arrived at Scott's home he was blasted with greetings and applause. Although he'd invited half the guests himself, he pretended to be taken by surprise. Diane, who had quickly noted my immediate confusion (the glare of lights eliminated even peripheral vision), came across to me and suggested I might be more comfortable in the less crowded den. From the doorway she introduced me to about eight guests whose names, with a couple of exceptions, meant nothing to me. Then she spoke the name of Jim Brock!

Jim Brock! I spun back in memory to my high school days. I could see a shy, boyish face. I'd had such a crush on him. His father had owned and had recently sold one of the biggest department stores in the city.

I must have made some sound, because Diane paused in her

introductions and said, "Oh, so you do remember Jim?" Her question was answered by Jim himself.

"I'd be more than a little put out if she didn't," he said. Then obviously speaking to the whole company, he added, "Know where and when I last saw Joan?"

"You're about to tell us," said Diane.

"She was dancing on a table at the senior wingding—the senior all-night party after our graduation."

"Nonsense, Jim," I shouted. "I never."

"Did you ever!" he responded.

"And you, James Brock, walked away when I was going to have you sign my yearbook."

"Well, that was a big mistake," he said, laughing.

Everyone in the den was enjoying this exchange.

The next moment Jim was beside me. Scott, who'd been Jim's college roommate, must have told him about my loss of sight, because he maneuvered me around furniture.

"Come and sit on a cushion by the fire," he said. "We've a lot of catching up to do."

That was an understatement. We barely moved from the den's fireplace for the next four hours. Most of our early dialogue was on the "do you remember?" plane, and we ran through names of students who'd been in our class.

For me it was a significant and revealing interlude when Scott's two very young daughters, one in pajamas and one in a nightgown, bounded into the den and made straight for "Uncle Jim." He tickled them into squeals and giggles and allowed them to bounce on his stomach. They obviously adored him.

After Diane had pulled them away and packed them off to bed, Jim said, "I'm not their uncle, of course, but I'm never happier than when playing the role. I just love kids."

What also impressed me was the quiet and natural way Jim kept me informed on what was going on. I learned from him why, for example, there was an explosion of laughter when Scott opened a birthday gift of a toilet paper holder which, when the paper was pulled, played Scottish bagpipes. He named for me the guests as they entered the room, and he kept me supplied with snacks, including cocktail sausages on toothpicks.

Then Jim and I found ourselves approaching graver issues. I told him of my sadness on hearing of the death in an auto accident of his sister Lori, who, although my senior by three years, had been my friend.

"It was a long time ago, but I still miss her," Jim said. "I always will."

"Lori had just everything going for her," I said softly. "I remember how she was homecoming queen, cheerleader, and so wonderfully spirited." I touched Jim's arm as I added, "I guess there could have been a more appropriate time than a birthday party to speak of your sister, but I never did get the chance to talk to you when she died. I was in college in South Dakota at the time."

There was a moment and then Jim asked, "Is it the wrong time, then, to talk about what happened to you? The amazing thing is, Joan, that you don't look as if you've had bad things happen to you. Mind my saying this? Truthfully, I was absolutely amazed when Diane brought you into this room."

I tried to brush away this unexpected compliment. "What did you expect—a depressed widow bumping into the furniture?"

His laugh held no more humor than mine when he said, "Perhaps someone like that."

For the first time since we'd started to talk (was it really two hours earlier?) there was a shared sense of moving from safe shallows into deeper water. Jim broke the moment by rising to his feet and taking my wineglass. He murmured something about recharging at the wet bar. His leaving the room gave me an excuse to freshen up in the bathroom. Diane had pointed out its door when she had led me to the den.

I was in no hurry. I needed the pause, perhaps to check on or even to rein in feelings that were stirring in those areas of my mind and heart that had not been opened for a very long time.

I felt really frustrated that I was unable to age by twenty years that boyish face in high school.

On my returning to the fireplace, from which, as far as I could tell, came the only light in the den, I held out my hand for the refilled glass. The low light gave me a little peripheral vision.

Jim said, "I thought you were supposed to be blind!"

I smiled as I sat on the floor cushion beside him.

"Of course," I said, "you're wondering how I navigated? Well, once I've walked through a room I know what to avoid. How did I know you were here and offering me a full glass? With my peripheral vision I saw white blobs on the floor. I recognized the blobs as your white tennis shoes, and it was pretty safe to presume that you'd returned from the bar with replenished glasses. It was easy, you see."

He clinked his glass to mine and said, "I'm impressed." He was fun, comfortable. I liked this man.

"Now what about you?" I asked. "What do you do and how many wives have you had?"

I could almost hear his grin as he said, "As an astronaut I'm scheduled for next week's flight to Mars. I was able to get here tonight only because there's been a leak in one of the booster rockets. Wives? Henry the Eighth ain't got nothing on me."

I dug my elbow into his ribs. "The truth," I demanded, "or I shall drive myself home."

Both of us were again enjoying the safe banter.

"I'm a lepidopterist," he said.

"That," I responded, "sounds like a word in a crossword puzzle or a spelling bee. You're either an authority on Bohemian art or you extract perfume from exotic flowers."

Jim slapped a thigh. "You're not all that far off," he said. "A lepidopterist is a student of butterflies, and butterflies are drawn to flowers by their scents and colors."

"So you spend your time catching butterflies!" I exclaimed. "I'm somehow getting the wrong picture. The one I'm getting is like a *New Yorker* cartoon. There's a guy with knobby knees waving a little green net on the end of a stick."

He chuckled. "Well, I don't have knobby knees and I look for butterflies in places like Brazilian rain forests and the West Indies. Also in Arizona, where I live now. Do you want me to go into details?"

"I'm already fascinated," I told him.

Jim went on to tell me that he had recently co-authored an authoritative illustrated book on butterflies at his home in Tucson.

As he spoke, I was gaining a better picture of the man. I'd known him to be a wit and I now knew him to be a scientist; I was also seeing him as a passionate lover of nature. He spoke urgently of the need to preserve nature's threatened treasures.

I was really listening and being much intrigued by his intensity when he suddenly stopped in mid-sentence. "Oh, heck!" he exclaimed, "I didn't mean to have tunnel vision when I got onto butterflies. I don't want to scare you off."

"Do I look scared?" I asked.

"You look—you look—well, much prettier than anything I've ever encountered in the forests of Brazil."

I gave Jim my most dazzling smile and told him that this was the most original compliment I'd ever been given. I added, "But I can't wait to hear about your love life."

"You're going to have to wait," he said, "'cause we're all but the last people to go home. If we don't move out now Scott and Diane will boot us out."

I told him that I couldn't leave until Scott was ready to take me home. I held my breath, hoping that this hint was strong enough for Jim to offer to drive me home himself. We'd walked out of the den and were now near the front door. When Jim didn't respond to the hint, I was tempted to ask him plainly if he would drive me home.

My timidity prevailed. The opportunity was quite lost when Diane embraced me and Scott led me to his car. There was not even an opportunity to say goodnight to my stimulating companion of the evening.

On the five-mile drive home I casually asked Scott if his longtime friend had ever been married.

"Surprisingly not," said Scott. "Of course, now that Jim lives in Arizona—that's where he got his degree in biology—I don't see much of him. Before he graduated he worked for his father in the department store for three or four years. I wasn't married then and we had some great times together. He was never short of a date. One of his girls—forget her name—went on to do quite well in Hollywood. No, I think Jim's been totally wrapped up in his specialty. He must have told you about the butterflies. Gather he's quite a significant name in lepidopterology. He's done what so many wished they had done. He's followed his dream. He's a nice guy."

"Yes," I agreed, "he's a very nice guy." I was glad Scott had no reason to feel my pulse.

When Louise and Sandy dropped in for coffee the next morning they quickly picked up on my enthusiasm.

"Not Jim Brock!" exclaimed Louise. "When I was in junior college he was just about the number one catch."

"Right," joined in Sandy. "Most everyone bought their clothes at Brock's. Believe his folks also have a beautiful place on the beach somewhere."

I told Louise and Sandy as much as I'd learned about Jim, but bewailed my low expectation of ever being likely to see him again.

Both took me to task, Sandy saying, "Joan, haven't you heard? This is the nineties! We gals are allowed to phone up the guys and ask for dates."

"Oh, I just couldn't do it," I told them. Then an inspired thought hit me. I could ask Jim about publishing a book. That, after all, was what I was hoping to do myself sometime. I shared this notion with my friends and explained how Jim had authored and published an important volume.

Over our coffee mugs the strategy was laid out. I managed to find the Brocks' unlisted number through phoning Scott. Jim was not at home when I called, but his father was, and he promised to deliver my message and my phone number to his son.

Thus it was on the last day of 1991 that Jim Brock took me to lunch at a Bakersfield restaurant called the Olive Garden. Later I was to reflect that the very first love story also began in a garden.

16

From the Desert with Love

§

This is a letter I audiotaped to Cathy on January 18, 1992:

... There's a man in my life!! Oh Cathy, my dear, I can hear
your cry of alarm. Is it for real? I don't know. I mean, I wake up
with my heart singing and I go to bed with mosquitoes of doubt
buzzing and stinging my mind. I tell myself that it can't be, that it
couldn't be. This happiness I've dreamed about, this gift I've prayed
for, is surely not for me.

What I'm attempting to tell you, Cathy, is that I'm trying to
be cautious. I tell myself, Joan, just you remember who you are!
You can't even see his face. You can't run into his arms without
tripping over the doormat. You can't . . . you can't . . . you can't!

But I did see his face—twenty years ago. We were in high
school together, same class. I can still see the boy smile but not the
man. Yet I hear his words and I feel his touch.

But I can tell you the split second when the beautiful thing happened, the moment when we put music to our words. We were having lunch at this restaurant which was almost deserted because I guess everyone was preparing to see in the New Year.

So we had the place to ourselves, and we sat in a booth. I should have told you that we'd met two nights earlier at the birthday party of a mutual friend. There, at the friend's home, we talked for about four hours, tapping into each other's life experiences, discovering each other's laughter buttons. There were some sad reflections, too. But I liked him almost at once. In fact, I liked him very much.

His name's Jim (yes, another "J" in my life!). Then, the morning after the party, Louise and Sandy worked out an excuse for Jim to invite me to lunch (what a web we women can weave!).

He's a scientist—actually an authority on butterflies. He calls himself a lepidopterist. Glad I'm taping and not writing this letter to you 'cause I'm not sure of the spelling. Look it up in your *Webster's*.

Where was I? Ah, yes, in a booth of this almost empty restaurant toying with wineglasses (we had both ordered and eaten quiche—one of the easier dishes for me to handle), when suddenly—yes, this is when it happened—his hand came across the table and rested on mine.

Fireworks? No! Electric storm? No. Did the aspen leaves tremble? No! But something I don't know how to describe passed from his hand to mine. He'd touched me before, of course. He'd led me from my front door to his car, for example. He had guided me to our table. Our hands had touched when he'd passed me the pepper and the bread rolls. But this on-the-table touch was different.

Actually, after his hand had been resting on mine for some seconds he asked, "Is it okay for me to do this?"

I nodded, and my smile widened. I know you'll understand, Cathy, when I tell you that it was not only a physical but—well—a sort of spiritual connection. It was as if it was planned by You Know Who.

We're not teenagers. That meeting of the sensitive skins of our fingers was far, far removed from two kids holding sticky hands in the back seats of a movie theater, or the first kisses in Dad's Buick. Back then (as you, too, will remember) it was all breathless, and a bit scary.

At this restaurant I knew what was going through my mind, but I could only guess at what was going through his. What we said to each other was not so important. We did discuss his authorship of a book, and I told him of my literary ambitions. We got into philosophical areas after I'd asked him how he had developed his interest in butterflies. He was ballistically enthusiastic when he spoke about his awe on first watching at the age of seven a butterfly emerge from a chrysalis.

I murmured the first lines of that hymn we all sang in Sunday school:

> *All things bright and beautiful,*
> *All creatures great and small . . .*

To my surprise and delight, Jim recited the last lines!

> *All things wise and wonderful,*
> *The Lord God made them all.*

"So you believe in God?" I asked him.

He replied, "Not many realize that Charles Darwin held a very strong belief in God. So did Einstein, for that matter. Anyone who has looked through a microscope at the wings of a butterfly or who has seen, as I have, a butterfly with a two-inch, azure-blue wingspan settle on the petal of an orchid in the Brazilian rain forests does not have to be persuaded that God exists, and that His creative and unparalleled artistry is evident everywhere." He made the phrases sound much lighter than they do when I try to recall them.

We finger-tipped the rim of our beliefs because our dialogue was more of a reconnaissance of each other's likes, dislikes, hopes, and creeds than a full exploration.

Heck, Cathy, what I'm trying to tell you—because I know you'll be happy for me but anxious, too—is that both Jim and I understand that not only is something wonderful happening to us, but that both of us must weigh the obvious problems and difficulties.

We're told that love is blind, but when one of the lovers is actually without sight, the warnings to go carefully are, or should be, red-lettered.

For me, the strongest of these warnings is whether Jim really understands what he might be getting into. There'll soon be an opportunity for us to talk at a deeper level because—guess what?— he's given me a very unusual birthday present, a round-trip plane ticket to Tucson, Arizona, where he's lived for the past fifteen years. Southern Arizona happens to be just about the best area in the country for the study of butterflies. This may be irrelevant trivia to you, but it's no longer trivia to me!

Since that luncheon on New Year's Eve, and his return to his Tucson home, we've talked for about a hundred hours on the phone. I hope you've got some stock in AT&T (or is it Sprint?) because the dividends should be soaring! You might also invest in Interflora, because long-stemmed roses are arriving by the dozens!

Jim's just been to Jamaica (on butterfly business), and I've just returned from a two-day visit to Sacramento (medical checkup and a talk to a women's conference put on by Clemson University). The phone calls were uninterrupted and the local florist shop is still delivering.

Cathy, do you smell smoke? If so, it's because my birthday present from Jim—the plane ticket to Tucson—is probably scorching the envelope in the second drawer down on the right side of my dresser!

Now, what are you thinking? What I believe I could hear you saying—or what I would like to hear you saying—is that if Jim really cares for me he will protect me better than he would guard the rarest of his butterflies.

Sounds like a quote from an Elizabeth Barrett Browning poem to her beloved Robert. Remember it? "How do I love thee? Let me count the ways . . . " We had to learn it by heart when I was in tenth grade.

Jim hasn't actually said that he loves me. These words need the right setting, don't they? What he did say in an earlier phone call was, "Joan, we need time alone with each other. You need to know who I am." I was really deeply touched that he was thinking of me and my concerns in this way. He knows there are big questions on my mind, not the least of them being Joy's well-being.

He and Joy took to each other from the moment they first met. After her second meeting with Jim she said, "Mom, he's real neat and he makes me laugh." I don't need to tell you that "neat" is currently the ultimate tribute of a ten-year-old. My parents also gave Jim their immediate approval. "Very interesting and courteous young man," huffed Dad. "Too few like 'em around these days." If Dad hadn't guessed I was in love, Mom surely did. I'm sure she was winking when she said, "I like him very much."

Cathy, please forgive me, as I know you will, for a taped letter that's all about the very special him. Greet the other girls for me and, of course, Dennis.

Much love from my song-filled heart,

Joan

Three days after mailing this tape, I received a cryptic telegram that read: CHECKED LEPIDOPTERIST. VINTON FRIENDS FEEL YOUR HEART IS GIVING GOOD SIGNALS. NEED PROGRESS REPORTS. LOVE CATHY ET AL.

Cathy's telegram made me glow because I knew her to be blessed with good intuition.

At the end of January, my heart was still song-filled, but there was a timorous quaver to the top notes as the airplane nosed down to the runway in Tucson. Although Arizona bordered California, surprisingly I had never visited the state. A sad thought flashed through my mind—I'd never actually see the famous saguaros, the multilimbed cactuses made known to the world through Western movies, and which stand like sentinels across the desert landscape.

Earlier in the flight I had asked a stewardess to check my makeup. She told me what I'd been told before—that I barely needed any and that I looked just fine.

"Meeting someone important?" she asked, and I knew her eyebrows were near her hairline.

I nodded.

"Then I'll be meeting him, too," she said, "because I'll be taking you off the plane." She laughed. "But you needn't worry. I'm no competition." Another laugh. "But who would be?" (Parenthetically, here, I want to say that in all my traveling—and I've traveled continents since setting out to write this story—every flight attendant has treated me like a favorite sister.)

The real reason I was edgy was not that I'd overdone the eye shadow, but that I'd be meeting Jim on his home ground.

Oh, we'd spoken half a million words on the phone, but we'd not seen each other in several long weeks. He'd surely find out now how much I'd depend on him, not only to guide my steps, but for descriptions of everything that was going on around me.

In our last phone conversation he'd mentioned that he'd gotten tickets for a basketball game. I'd enjoyed playing basketball myself at college, and I knew the rules and skills. But if I were to become involved in the game he'd have to be a radio commentator. Would he weary of this and other tasks?

The wheels of the plane touched the runway, lifted for a couple of seconds, then touched again. The intercom speaker above my head welcomed us to Tucson and warned passengers not to move until the airplane had come to a complete standstill.

Inside my head a voice was saying, "You're crazy, Joan. You're trying to live out a dream. Wake up. What are you really doing here?" My pulse was hitting the high numbers. I wondered if the passenger next to me could hear it.

The airplane came to a halt at the terminal. The stewardess came to me. She reached up to pull my carry-on bag from the overhead locker. She said brightly, "Well, here we are. Give me your hand. I'll take you off ahead of the other passengers. Excited?"

A minute later I heard a familiar and loved voice. It said, "You look beautiful, Joan. I'm so happy you're here." His arms were around me. His lips touched mine. I heard him thank the stewardess. Then he pressed a rose into my hands. It was sealed into a thin vial of water.

He said, "I felt pretty goofy holding this flower, but since you grasped it, the petals have started to open up." He laughed. I loved his laugh; all my earlier nervous feelings lifted like a sea mist touched by the sun.

The other passengers were now coming off the airplane. I could hear them moving around me. They may have wondered what was going on as they saw a woman with a cane holding the elbow of a man who, so he told me, was "one big grin."

As I allow my mind to savor again the memories of my first visit to Tucson, Arizona, I'm getting goose bumps. I'm like a kid on her first trip to the beach—all delight and bewilderment and fascination.

Yes, we went to the university basketball game where Jim proved to be an excellent commentator. Yes, we went to a marvelous restaurant in the foothills. We drove above the snowline of Mount Lemmon, where we pelted each other with snowballs. I have proof of this because everywhere we went Jim recorded our activities on his video camera. Obviously my snowballs went wide of their mark, but every now and then Jim pretended (I'm sure) that I'd hit my target. The snowballs that hit me were powder-puff soft. Our laughter echoed off the cliffs.

He explained his reason for making the video movie. "I don't forget," he said, "that I'm courting two blondes. These pictures are for Joy."

When later, back in Bakersfield, I ran the tape through my TV, it wasn't the snowball fight that gave Joy her biggest laugh. What sent her into hysterics were shots taken by me. High up on Mount Lemmon, Jim had put the video camera into my hands and had instructed me to pan across the valley far below. Unable to observe what I was shooting, the camera had tilted right and left. The outcome, Joy told me, was like flying in a small plane that was doing aerobatics!

Joy was quite enchanted by another shot, this of a butterfly emerging from its chrysalis. Jim had been waiting for the emerging of the butterfly for two years! He had kept the chrysalis in his small laboratory.

The close-up tripod shot showed the butterfly on his hand as it unfolded and dried off its exquisite wings. I quote from Jim's running commentary given on the day of my arrival!

"Is the analogy too obvious?" Jim had asked.

Laughingly I told him that I'd set a limit on the number of times he could refer to me as "one of his bugs"! I was discovering, though, that he was a poet at heart, as I suppose is everyone who glories in the beauty of nature.

Within a few hours of the hatching of the butterfly, which was indigenous to southern Arizona, we drove eight miles into the desert to release it among the flora upon which it fed. While we traveled he played on the car's tape recorder the theme song from that classic movie, *Born Free*.

In the mid-morning of the third day of my four-day visit to Arizona, Jim told me to close my eyes.

"Close my eyes!" I exclaimed, laughing. "You mock me, sir!"

"I mock thee not," he said. "I've ordered up the magic carpet. It will take us to a place of enchantment."

Outside, the air was cool, but the desert sun was warm upon my face. There was a delicate aroma of what Jim informed me was a creosote bush. "Have we already arrived?" I asked as I spread my arms.

"You haven't even gotten aboard," he replied before leading me to his four-wheel-drive truck, which had enormous wheels. He needed this vehicle for climbing mountains, he had told me— "and to go today where no man hath gone before," he added. He played the innocent when I accused him of pinching that line from *Star Trek*.

Shortly, we were rumbling along on our way, and within thirty minutes of our setting out we were obviously off the beaten track for I was being tossed about like a cork in a boiling cauldron. Through chattering teeth I told him that his magic carpet was badly in need of a lube job.

Eventually he pulled the truck to a stop, turned off the

engine, and leaned across to open the passenger door. I heard the sound of tumbling water. As he helped me to the ground he instructed me to use my imagination.

"It may sound like a waterfall to you," he said, "but what you hear are tiny violins being played by red-capped elves sitting cross-legged on toadstools. They've been given a Sunbelt vacation by Santa after their hard work at Christmas." He left me for a moment as he pulled some things from the back of the truck. One was a blanket, the other a picnic basket.

He spread the blanket on what he told me (and I should have guessed by the fresh and distinctive smell) was a carpet of pine needles. He ordered me to lie down and test it for comfort.

"Not exactly an innerspring," I told him, "and there's a little lumpy thing in the small of my back."

When he had removed what he told me was a small pine cone, he suggested that in some previous incarnation I had probably been that princess who had complained about a pea under ninety-nine mattresses.

We enjoyed a long moment, stretching our limbs, breathing deeply of the purest air, now pine scented. I was aware, too, of a breeze moving the leaves of other trees and shrubs on the mountain slope.

"Yes," he said eventually, "this is why I love this country. I've come here often simply to enjoy a sense of freedom and space. You could believe that concrete and crowds and man's despoiling of the good earth are on another planet. Here you can whisper, or shout for joy or speak of gracious things. Do you wonder that this is where I seek butterflies?"

He stirred. The pine needles under his prone body whispered. Then, because of the sudden loss of sunlight, I was aware of the shadow of his head above me. I didn't move. There hadn't been a moment since I'd lost my sight that I had more desired to see. His fingers combed my hair and he kissed me very tenderly.

I had guessed that this time would come. I had played it out in my mind—not quite like this, not in this magical place. I had known that I would have to freeze the frame, to stop the movement of the scene until I'd spoken lines that might risk my losing Jim.

I pressed my hands into his shoulders, and as soon as my lips were freed I said quietly, "Jim, I must talk. I need to talk about things that I don't want to tell you."

He pulled away from me, arching his back. "Then don't tell me," he said. "Just listen to the elves on their violins. Are they playing *allegro, animato,* or *dolce?*"

"I'm not completely with you," I said.

"Just testing your knowledge. A concert pianist friend has been trying to educate me in classical music. Allegro means brisk, animato is lively, and dolce is—oh, you can guess that one—it means gentle or sweetly. What do you hear, Joan?"

"Forgot to tell you I had piano lessons," I said, "but the music I hear now is in the words of a man I've grown to love."

He drew in a deep breath. "And I'm looking down on the loveliest face I've ever seen. I love that face. I love the one whose face it is."

He bent his head to kiss me again. But once more I put more pressure on his shoulders. "Oh, Jim," I murmured, "my heart aches for you, my mind, my spirit too. But I have to talk to you about something that's really important."

He picked up the gravity of my voice. There was a long moment before he rolled away from me and lay on his back.

This small separation hurt. I couldn't be sure that he was still looking at me. The glare of the sky obliterated all peripheral vision.

Almost choking, I said, "There can be nothing more wonderful than to love and be loved. But I'm afraid, Jim, so afraid . . . "

"Of me?"

"No, no, not of you. Not of a man who takes a butterfly eight miles for its supper."

"Then?"

I was silent, but trying hard to force words from a throat that wouldn't immediately release them.

Jim said gently, "Would it help if I held your hand?"

"Yes, it would help," I managed to say. His hand held mine and his fingers were busy in my palm. Strength that had ebbed seemed to flow back to me. I found that I was able to speak calmly, logically.

"We're not really children at play," I said. "We're both grown-ups, Jim, and we must think and act like adults. Not far from this peaceful, beautiful place there are supermarkets where, I suspect, you bought the cold cuts or whatever, the bread and the coffee that you have in the picnic basket. Have you thought that when I go to a grocery store I am unable to select from a shelf one can of soup or one bottle of soy sauce? There are cars out there on the highways and freeways—millions of them. Have you thought that I cannot drive even one of them? There are schools and dentists' offices. Have you thought that I cannot take my daughter to school and I cannot take her to a park? When I'm in a home and someone leaves a closet door open I can hurt myself. I live in a world of glare or twilight. I've lived in this world for eight years. Whatever more years are given to me are going to be lived out in this shadowed world. Have you really thought about this, Jim? Believe me, I'm not being self-pitying. I've accepted this unseeing world of mine. I'm no heroine but I've not been unhappy in it."

Jim made no attempt to interrupt me, and I was grateful that he didn't. I was grateful, too, for the touch of his fingers on my palm.

I surprised myself by the steadiness of my voice. I could have been speaking about the weather or a bus timetable. Yet I was aware that what I was saying could end a glorious love affair.

After taking some moments to regather thoughts I continued, "You asked me, Jim, what I'm afraid of. By now, you surely know what it is but I'll spell it out for you. I'm afraid that you will tire of me—perhaps not of me, but of what living with me would be like—not now, not for a few days, not for a few months, but in a year, five years, ten years. Yes, this thought makes me afraid for you, afraid for myself."

My voice trailed into silence. The only sound now came from the waterfall close by. I could no longer picture Jim's elves sitting cross-legged on toadstools. I tried to create an image of his expression. Were the lips that had kissed me so tenderly a few minutes earlier now grimly tightened? Was his jaw working?

Suddenly he drew his hand away from mine. The pine needles under the blanket rustled again. I knew he was now sitting up.

My heart turned over.

The sky's glare was shadowed over once again, and I was aware that he was looking down at me. Was he adding up the cost of my speaking the truths he needed to hear?

A moment—a long moment during which my thoughts moved from agony to sublime elation—for his lips were upon mine once more.

After the long kiss I whispered, "Oh, Jim, I thought I'd lost you. I thought . . . "

"Joan, you still don't know who I am," he said. His voice was light, touched by laughter. "Do you believe that I haven't given a lot of thought to what you've spoken about? Don't you understand my love for you?"

Then, "I don't claim all the virtues, Joan, but a man who chases butterflies has to have lots and lots of patience. You spoke about the years ahead. Didn't I tell you that the butterfly which emerged from its chrysalis yesterday had kept me waiting for two years? When I'm searching for a particular caterpillar or chrysalis I spend hours, days, sometimes even a week on my knees searching through clumps of grass. When I'm in the rain forests of Brazil I can spend a month looking for a metal mark butterfly, a critter smaller than a dime that helps to maintain the balance of nature, an incredible living thing that perhaps only one person in a hundred would notice, even if it was in front of their nose."

He kissed me again before he continued. "I've been waiting years for a wife. I've been lonely for far too long. Every Christmas my mother has asked me what I want for a gift. Every year for the past decade I've told her I want a wife. It's a family joke. Do you know what she gave me this Christmas? A sheepskin coat. Nice—but not a wife. Patience! Gosh, Joan, do I have patience! Then I met beautiful you!"

I was listening to a naturalist's soliloquy. In the event that I might interrupt him, I bit my lip. He, too, took pause for breath, then continued. "Now I can tell you what happened after we had our lunch on New Year's Eve. I went back to my mother and I told her that I'd found her—found the woman I want to marry. I didn't tell her more than that. I didn't even tell her your name, because I wasn't sure that the woman I'd found would want me—yes, me, Jim Brock, a forty-year-old bachelor who seeks rare butterflies! But on the off chance that she might agree to marry me I asked my mother for advice on buying an engagement ring. Mother went to her bedroom wall safe and came back not with a ring, but this."

Jim now uncurled the fingers of my left hand and placed within my palm what felt like a hard, thin, little stick. He closed my fingers around it.

Up to this point I'd been speechless, but now I asked, "What is it, Jim? What is this?"

"Hold on to it tightly," he instructed. "It's probably just as hard to find a diamond stickpin among pine needles as it is to find a needle in a haystack."

"It isn't really a diamond?" I exclaimed.

As I tightened my grip he hooted with laughter and said, "I guess this proposal is a first of its kind. You're holding my great aunt Sadie's diamond stickpin. I gather she wore it on her shoulder when she entertained President Theodore Roosevelt—someone like that. I'll re-check the family archives."

"Oh, Jim," I cried, "I'm trying to keep up with you. You have to be kidding!"

"No, it's true, more or less," he said. "The pin is eighty years old, and the diamond was created when God said, 'Let there be light.' Oh, and by the way, I'm asking you to marry me. If your answer is yes, we'll find a jeweler, to put Aunt Sadie's diamond into an engagement ring."

"Oh, Jim! Jim!"

"That's okay," he said, laughing. "You don't have to hurry with your answer. You can think about it over a lunch of chicken breasts and potato salad. I brought half a dozen napkins, too. You can use one of them to wipe away a smear on your left cheek. I think it's a mix of sand, wild grass seeds, and a saline solution."

While we ate lunch I told him I could indeed now hear his cross-legged elves playing their violins.

"Allegro, animato, or dolce?" he asked.

"All three." I replied, laughing. "And what perfect harmony!"

17

Twilight also Heralds Dawn

§

An audiotaped letter to Cathy, dated August 7, 1992:

. . . Oh, my dear Cathy, how to begin to tell you what's happened since I was last in touch? Where to find the words to describe my elation? Willy Shakespeare, where are you when I need you!

I've not even had the chance to talk to you about the wedding. Jim and I were married on June 27 in the small Bakersfield church where I was baptized and confirmed. There, at Sunday school and through my teenage years, I sang a thousand hymns, prayed ten thousand prayers.

Dad married us. Louise, the closest friend of my childhood—and indeed, of all my years—was my maid of honor. The Joy of my own bones and my flesh was the only bridesmaid.

The congregation was small because we'd invited only Jim's family and my own to witness the plighting of our troth.

Don't you love the word "troth"? It seems to embrace fidelity, care, and foreverness, and it comes, I'm sure, from the Middle Ages.

What did I wear? I'll not waste time describing the dresses because I'll be sending pictures taken by brothers Bob, who came from Virginia, and Jon. We've got the whole thing on videotape, too.

I had so many memorable moments. The first was coming down the aisle on Dad's arm. Dad's so frail these days. He's undergone major surgery on a heart that's spent nearly half a century giving its best to the spiritual and emotional needs of others.

While he was giving us his message, he choked up several times. Our wedding, I'm thinking, may be the last church rite that Dad is likely to perform. I kind of sense this, and I think he did too, as he asked his only daughter and the man at her side "to have and to hold from this day forward, for better, for worse, for richer, for poorer, in sickness and in health, until death us do part."

I was in a sort of daze of delight and my emotional Basque maid of honor wept through the exchange of vows. Afterward Dad laughingly reminded Louise that she was at a wedding, not a funeral!

Dad began by greeting us with the words, "Who can deny the Providence of God in bringing the two of you together?"

Not me, Cathy! I can remember Dad saying, "You, Joan, and you, James (he's always formal at baptisms, weddings, and funerals), will be walking the remainder of your journey in companionship, bearing each other's burdens, comforting one another, forsaking all others."

For me the most poignant moment was when Dad said, "Joan, you've had your share of pain, but never forget the words from the catechism that 'without the will of My Father in Heaven, not a hair shall fall from my head.'" His voice cracked for a moment before he added, "Hold fast to this, my beloved daughter Joan."

Last week when we ran through the video I couldn't help but think that every couple planning divorce should be obliged to sit down together and play back their wedding, listening again to the solemn and wonderful words they said to each other in front of minister, priest, or rabbi. Of course, the divorce lawyers would lobby like mad against such a law, but I'd bet that many marriages would be pulled back from the brink.

I'm meandering, as I usually do when I've got forty-five minutes of audiotape to play with. Now where was I? I'd left Jim at the altar (ha! ha!). No, Jim and I had said our I do's and he had kissed me (a long and lovely kiss), and I'm now wearing his gold ring alongside Great Aunt Sadie's diamond. The diamond is not as big as the one Richard Burton gave Elizabeth Taylor, but it's created a lot of oohs and aahs from girlfriends.

When Louise had stopped crying I was able to tell her how much her friendship had meant to me. Since we returned to Bakersfield, Louise has often been my right arm and my eyes and my confidante. She's driven Joy and me all the way to Pismo several times and she would have driven us to Timbuktu if I'd asked her. She drove Jim and me down to the Los Angeles airport where we boarded a plane for Hawaii. It's the first time I've ever turned left when boarding a plane. Stewardesses served us lunch on white linen—champagne, shrimp, and broiled peacock tongues! (Just kidding.)

Thus to our deluxe condo right on a beach in Maui. How close to paradise! Going to sleep on the shoulder of a man I love with all my heart, and to the surging sound of surf less than a hundred yards from our pillow.

Soon after we got back to Bakersfield we held our wedding reception. This was for friends and relatives from all over. We did invite you and Dennis, as you'll remember, and we were sorry you couldn't make it. But one very special guest was Jay, now athletically handsome and in his mid-teens. We flew him down from Iowa. By the way, while we were on our honeymoon Joy flew up to South Dakota to have time with Joe's folks. So all was, as usual, perfectly timed.

Then the big move to Tucson. I'd gotten rid of some of my furniture from the Bakersfield condo. Even so, Jim's big truck was loaded to the gunnels (whatever gunnels are). My precious talking computer and Visual Tek were padded by cushions. Guess we looked like one of the Dust Bowl families in a scene out of *Grapes of Wrath*.

Cathy, where are you when you actually listen to my audiotapes? If you're sensible, you're lying in a hot bath after your kids have gone to bed!

Another little miracle of nature! I didn't see it myself (naturally), but it sure excited Jim and Joy. We were on the outskirts of Tucson when there was a rainstorm. Although we'd roped a tarp over the furniture and other things in the back of the truck, I was nervous about my computer getting wet. So Jim pulled the truck under a railroad bridge. After the brief storm was over and as we were emerging from the bridge Jim and Joy hollered.

"Stop screaming," I shouted. "What's happening?"

"It's a rainbow!" yelled Joy.

"So what?" I said. "It's not the first rainbow you've seen."

"But, Mom, it's the brightest rainbow I've ever seen. It's unreal!"

Then Jim added, "The apex of the rainbow is right over my house—our new home."

Now I understood the reason for their excitement.

Jim pulled the truck to the side of the road to watch and describe this brilliant bow over our new home, all of us awestruck.

That night when Jim and I were in bed he brought up the subject of the rainbow again. He whispered, almost shyly, "I'm remembering your first visit to Tucson, honey, and how that butterfly chose the time of your arrival to emerge from its chrysalis. And today we're greeted by the mother and father of all rainbows! Been thinking of the words your Dad said at our wedding, that Providence brought us together. Nature's sure giving us a thumbs up."

This was my husband, the poet, speaking while his arms were around me. He wasn't laughing, Cathy—not this time.

What went through my mind was the story of the first rainbow. I'm pretty sure it's in Genesis, chapter nine, where God said to Noah that he had set a rainbow in the sky as a covenant that the days of tribulation were over. That's the gist of the story, I think. Look it up sometime.

So here I am, Cathy, lying in Jim's arms and with my heart overflowing with thankfulness, hope, and love, and thinking, I'm oh, so blessed. It was one incredibly beautiful moment.

To Jim I murmured, "So many memories."

My poetical husband replied, "So many wonderful memories yet to be made."

Now, Cathy, if you are lying in your bath and this tape has been spinning away, the water's probably tepid. You can get out of the tub now and towel yourself dry, because I've updated you on what my French teacher would have called "les affaires d'amour"—at least the affairs of Mrs. James Brock. Please remember my new name when you next write.

Dear love to you, as always,

Joan

* * *

My affairs continued to be fun-filled, exciting, and unexpectedly dramatic.

The fun-filled facets of my new life were centered on our family. Jim, the former forty-year-old bachelor, has become not only a deeply caring husband but a deeply caring father.

As Joy was making the transition from childhood to her teenage years she found another father. She calls him Jim, which was fine with both of us. In her going to a new school in a new city, it was Jim who was at her shoulder as often as I. When it came to the need for help with homework, Jim was understandably a lot more helpful than I could be. Joy who, by necessity, had always been older than her years, is now an honor student. With the genes of her biological father, she is a very good athlete.

When Jim was "bug-hunting," as he usually called his professional work here in Arizona, we'd often travel as a threesome into the desert. Sometimes we'd turn these expeditions into a picnic. I'd be left in some sheltered spot to guard the provisions while Jim and Joy clambered over terrain I could not safely manage. We'd keep in touch through a superior set of walkie-talkies. They'd tell me where they were and what success they were having.

On one especially lovely juniper-tree-scented summer's morning, they'd left me within earshot of a mountain stream. My walkie-talkie buzzed me out of a daydream. Jim told me that he had just netted a butterfly, one that he had been looking for on the higher slopes, and that Joy had been the first to spot the critter.

Five minutes later my walkie-talkie buzzed again. I wasn't really fooled when a squeakily disguised voice wailed, "I'm a pretty blue and gray butterfly. I was fluttering along up here when a man and a girl caught me in a net and put me into a glass jar. Please tell them to let me outta here 'cause my boyfriend is waiting for me." A giveaway giggle exploded into Joy's laughing hysterically. For the next few minutes the air waves on the lower slopes of the Santa Catalina Mountains crackled with the sounds of merriment.

An hour later, husband and daughter—both as hungry and as thirsty as hunters should be—joined me for lunch. Laughter drowned the sound of running water and lasted through the family outing.

It was a good day for the captured butterfly, too. Before we left for home we voted unanimously in favor of letting it go free. Joy excitedly told me that it circled us three times before soaring into the blue.

Putting on her squeaky voice once more, Joy said, "Thank you very much. I just hope my boyfriend's still waiting for me. He promised to take me to a flutterby game tonight, and tomorrow we're going to look for a nice place to lay my eggs."

In 1993 there was another major event in my life. Richard Sullinger, who eighteen months earlier had first spoken to me about the Million Dollar Round Table, had kept in close touch. He had cautioned that the international organization received annually at least five hundred applications to speak at each convention—the next one to be held in Boston. I was still not putting much store in my chances when he, as chairman of the selection committee, insisted that I was a "serious candidate."

The process of being selected to speak at a convention is precise and traditional. The filtering out of potential speakers is on a global scale.

Another selection committee member, Mike Weintraub, flew to Tucson especially to hear me speak to (of all groups) a church congregation. Unbeknown to me, Mr. Weintraub arrived when I was already into my talk, and in order to catch his plane back to San Francisco he was obliged to leave before I had concluded. However, he left a business card with one of the ushers. On it he had written, "You're absolutely terrific!" I was bowled over because my talk had been tailored to meet the interests of a church group.

In March I was invited to travel to Chicago to try out for the Round Table's main platform, for which only fifteen speakers would be chosen for the five-day convention in midsummer.

Phone calls were coming in several times a week, some from people in a professional production company who helped me refine my talk, which had to be reduced to twenty minutes.

In the midst of these exciting days, Dad died. In my last phone conversation with him he said, "Joan, I am so very proud of you, so very happy for you."

Dad's death took the gleam and glitter off the thrill of the upcoming Chicago event. Jim helped me through my grieving. He reminded me again and again, lovingly but firmly, that life goes on.

One afternoon Jim said, "Joan, it's time for you to stop thinking of yourself. What would your father be wanting you to do?" When I continued to hunch my shoulders in grief, Jim said angrily, "I'm not going to sit here watching you go on like this." So saying, he left the house, slamming the front door behind him. One hour passed, two hours, three. My stomach churned.

When Jim eventually returned to the house, he held me tightly and said, "Joan, sweetheart, I promise I'll never, never, do that again."

Yet what he had done was precisely what I had needed. I pulled myself together and focused again on the great opportunity being given to me.

At the end of March I went alone to Chicago, where I was

treated like royalty. An enormous black limo met me at the O'Hare airport. I'd half expected Bob, the limo driver, to kiss my hand. As I sat back on the luxuriant leather cushions while we positively glided to the Hyatt Regency Hotel, I said aloud, "Oh, if only the girls back home could see me now!"

The hotel's bellhop took me to my suite and walked me around the furniture. I gaped like a country cousin on discovering a big screen TV, three telephones, and a bathtub I could have drowned in. I drew back the curtains and tried to imagine the view. I pretended I was looking at the Sears Tower, taller than New York's Empire State Building.

Since I had three hours to wait before attending a formal dinner, I spent the time bathing and phoning Jim, Joy, and Mom. Unfortunately, Louise was not at home, so I couldn't brag about the limo.

Mike Weintraub, whom I'd not yet met but to whom I had spoken many times on the phone since he had left me the "absolutely terrific" business card in the Tucson church, and Mickie Hoesly, a woman of exceptional warmth and charm, conducted me to the banquet dinner. Here I shook a lot of firm hands. Toasts were drunk to success.

The next day I was taken to a small theater within the hotel complex. Thankfully, I was free of nerves, even though I now knew that within an hour or two I could be sent back to Tucson with a "thanks for coming letter, but you're not quite what we need." Some of the other candidates were given this advice.

Without blushing and committing the sin of pride, I cannot repeat what Richard Sullenger said to me after my presentation. Suffice it to say that I was selected to speak in June in Boston on the main platform before five thousand top business executives from five continents.

The Million Dollar Round Table proved to be the start of my professional career as a public speaker. I stopped pinching myself only when I enlisted the help of Ione, my former Braille School colleague, now living in Tucson, to help me choose a dress for the big event. I'd made up my mind on the kind of dress I wanted. It had to be feminine but without being fussy. Ione and I found the dress in a Tucson store. It was an emerald green silk creation, long-sleeved and softly draped.

"Made solely for you," enthused Ione. "As you look now, the ancient Greek sculptors would have sought the most flawless marble to sculpt you wearing that dress."

I laughingly hushed Ione into curbing her enthusiasm.

Jim and Joy accompanied me to Boston. The production company had carefully worked out every detail of the presentation. The only piece of furniture on the stage would be a stool, upon which I could sit "if my legs became rubbery," said Mickie Hoesly. To make sure I found my way to the stool, they had, on Jim's suggestion, tacked down a strip of broad white tape stretching from the stage wing from which I would enter. My peripheral vision would allow me to follow the white tape to the stool.

I was behind the curtain, just off stage, as the emcee made his excellent and humorous introduction.

I accused Jim of feeding me butterflies for breakfast. "Can't you stop them fluttering in my stomach?" I pleaded.

Jim's light laughter helped, as did an encouraging peck on my cheek, and as did Joy's "Good luck, Mom."

I started walking along the taped pathway. The blazing spotlights seemed to be brighter than the Arizona sun. I was unable to see even one of the thousands of men and women out there in front of me. They had not been told that I was blind nor were they to learn this until I was five minutes into my speech. Two huge closed-circuit TV display screens on each side of the proscenium arch were blowing my image up to King Kong size.

In the course of the welcoming applause I asked myself what on earth was an ordinary woman, a preacher's daughter from Bakersfield, doing in this distinguished company. Determinedly, I put aside the alarming thought that ten thousand eyes were now focused on me, and ten thousand ears were awaiting my first words.

I've since reviewed the professionally produced film of my speech, and I've cringed at my occasional nervous giggles. I choked a couple of times—just for a second or two—when I spoke about the moment when Dr. Corbett had told me that the damage to my eyes was "irreversible," and when I spoke about Joe's valor.

"And now," I said in concluding, "I'd like to introduce you to my new husband, Jim, and to my daughter, Joy."

A moment more and they were there beside me—these two I loved above all others. A clatter of briefcases falling to the floor; applause surging toward me, a great wave of applause that went on and on and on.

Jim shouted into my ear, "They're on their feet. Everyone in this huge auditorium is standing up." Later someone said to me, "Joan, you just floated off that stage." This wasn't accurate. Jim and Joy led me carefully down the steps to our seats in the front row.

I was crying now, and without shame. This can't be for me! I thought. Perhaps the President of the United States has just arrived. Perhaps . . .

Jim had to shout again into my ear. "The TV cameras are still focused on you. Smile, for Pete's sake, smile!" I wiped my tears, which just went on flowing.

Mike Weintraub hugged me. Mickie Hoesly tearfully hugged

me. Unknown others hugged me. "Stand up again, Joan," they instructed. "Wave to them. They won't let you go." I obeyed. Applause surged once more.

Later I was told, with what truth I don't know, that it was the longest applause given to any speaker in the sixty-six years' existence of the Million Dollar Round Table convention. I can't think who held all those stopwatches!

Eventually the emcee was back at the microphone. He said, very simply, "Joan, you've just made five thousand new friends from all around the world."

Later, in other halls of the convention center, many of these new friends came to invite me to speak. I was given invitations to travel to and speak in cities across America. Invitations were given to me to speak in Australia, Canada, South Africa, and Asia.

Even as I now prepare to parcel up the manuscript of this book to mail it to my publishers in New York, I am still recovering from jet lag, for I've just returned from speaking engagements in Malaysia and Singapore.

My publishers tell me that before the year is out they will be taking me to the major cities of the United States to speak to many millions of my fellow countrymen and women—children, too, I hope.

What am I going to say? What I want to say—and so urgently—is that while none can know what challenges lie ahead, or how steep will be the path, how rough the terrain, how often we may fall and be hurt, we must not give up the striving.

In quiet moments I've recalled that mystical dream wherein I saw a steep mountain with its golden crest. In this dream—or in my recollection of it—the craggy, sunlit summit sometimes seems to have the form of a citadel there for my taking—so long as I have the humility to ask the Guide for His footholds and the courage to trust Him.

When we think of twilight, we think first of the mellow or sometimes melancholy hour that heralds night. We tend to forget that twilight also heralds the dawn.

In our journeying down the years not one of us can avoid those darkening times when the color of our lives bleeds to gray—times when we are shadowed or companioned by pain, fear, grief, or a sense of helplessness. Yet, as certain as the coming of every dawn, there's the hour when darkness breaks, when life itself is bright and colorful once more.

How often in my own dawn's brightenings has my heart cried out—sometimes, indeed, my throat and lips, "Ah there, up there, I see my pathway once again!"

And a Postscript

§

Tom Sullivan, my friend who has been a model and, indeed, a hero figure for those of us who are disabled, wrote an introduction to this book. It seems to me, then, not inappropriate that I end my story in his company once again.

Recently I was on a working visit to Los Angeles and was staying in the home of mutual friends. Tom and his lovely wife, Patty, were also dinner guests.

Our hostess, Erica, had provided a memorable meal during which much of the conversation across the dining table was about the loss of vision and how Tom and I had been compensated by the honing and heightening of our other senses. Surely, for instance, Tom's taste buds and my own gave us a gourmet's appreciation of the roast lamb.

We spoke, Tom and I, about our richer experiences of touch

and taste and scent and hearing. Perhaps we should not give away all our secrets, such as when Tom claimed, truthfully, I'm sure, that he could fairly accurately evaluate the personality of a stranger after a handshake—the limp ones disclose lack of confidence and the grip that lasts a few seconds longer than the norm indicates a welcome's warmth.

I talked about what a beach now means to me, of how much more I now valued the sounds and the smell of the ocean, the feel of the sand under my feet, and so on.

We differed on some issues, Tom and I. For instance, was it better (or tougher) to be born blind or to lose one's sight in mature years (images remembered or imagination?), but we found complete accord in believing that the passage of time is marked not only by hours and years but, so critically, by choices.

We both knew of people struck down by one misfortune or another who had elected lives of whimpering and self-pity. This was their free choice. We spoke of others who had chosen to use the hard knocks of life to grow, to achieve, and to find stimulating material and spiritual rewards.

We laughed, as did all the company, about our blunders and mishaps. Tom told an uproariously amusing story of how his seeing-eye dog had recently led him astray in San Antonio, Texas. The dog, Nelson, had been seduced by the odor of hot dogs being cooked on an open fire on a vacant lot by a group of hobos. Tom had sat down with the gentlemen of the road, had enjoyed a proffered hot dog, and had filed away yet another anecdote for his brilliant platform speeches.

Then, while we were enjoying an exotic dessert, I called home to Tucson on a speakerphone and brought Jim and Joy into our cheerful dining table conversation.

Toward the end of this exhilarating evening and while we

were now seated on deep, cushioned couches in a firelit living room, Tom turned to me and asked a penetrating question.

"Tell me," he said, "what is the difference between the Joan of ten years ago, the Joan who could see, and the Joan who is sitting next to me now?"

"I'm happier," I said without any hesitation.

"Happier!" exclaimed Tom, who had never seen his fingernails.

"Much, much happier," I assured him.

From a chair on the other side of the fireplace Patty said softly, "What a wonderful answer!"

"Oh, but it's true," I said. "In all my life I've never been happier—no never!"